SELECTED POEMS

SELECTED POEMS

VERN RUTSALA

ACKNOWLEDGEMENTS

The work in this book has been selected from these previously published books.

The Window, © 1959, 1960, 1962, 1963, 1964 by Vern Rutsala; Wesleyan University Press.

Laments, ©1975 by Vern Rutsala; New Rivers Press.

The Journey Begins, ©1976 by Vern Rutsala; The University of Georgia Press.

Paragraphs, © 1976 by Vern Rutsala; Wesleyan University Press.

Walking Home from the Icehouse, © 1981 by Vern Rutsala; Carnegie Mellon University Press.

Backtracking, © 1985 by Vern Rutsala; Story Line Press.

Ruined Cities, © 1987 by Vern Rutsala; Carnegie MellonUniversity Press.

A number of these poems appeared in chapbooks prior to their appearance in the books listed above. *The Mystery of Lost Shoes,* Lynx House Press, © 1985; *The New Life,* Trask House Books, © 1978; *The Harmful State,* The Best Cellar Press,© 1971; *Small Songs,* The Stone Wall Press, © 1969.

Grateful acknowledgement is made to those editors.

The author wishes to thank the Guggenheim Foundation and the National Endowment for the Arts for fellowships which enabled him to bring many of these poems into being.

Library of Congress Catalog Card Number:
90-52857

ISBN: 0-934257-52-3 (cloth)
ISBN: 0-934257-61-2 (paper)

Book design by Lysa McDowell

Published by Story Press, Inc.
d.b.a. Story Line Press
Three Oaks Farm
Brownsville, OR
97327-9718

Publication of this book was made possible by the generous support of the

Nicholas Roerich Museum, New York.

CONTENTS

from The Journey Begins

from Paragraphs

from Walking Home from the Icehouse

from Backtracking

from Ruined Cities

To Joan

THE WINDOW

Waking, afraid to touch
  the wound that morning
  has inflicted, we turn and
  lift the bandage of the blinds.
  Beyond the window
  wind-up birds totter
  seeming to listen to the grass.

In our yard the weeds
  are doing well and give
  their seeds to any wind
  that blows, even to our
  wordless neighbors who try,
  it seems, to set the world
  straight each day with hoes
  and hoses. Their hands
  are all green thumbs that
  test the pulse of twigs.

Sitting back, we watch their
  rituals of the spring.
  In clothing carefully aged
  they work and work
  prying flowers from their dirt
  or pinching bushes until
  the welts of buds appear.

Pausing, they scout
with glances the No Man's Land
of our yard which must
for them conceal mines;
or they long, perhaps,
to harness the worms
that wander our bloomless soil.

In the bands of shade
taped below the brims
of their straw hats,
their pious eyes float,
possibly irrigated by tears
for all our wild grass
that aches for the quick
teeth of a mower.
But they are busy people
and so they bend again
to tease color from their dirt.

Over what breakfast we find,
we watch them poke for frail
tendrils under stones
and imagine that they
dream all day of times
when they will pose,
sunburned and earthy,
beside their prize azaleas.
But our flowering weeds
bother them and we half-expect

to see them at night
quietly pawing our yard,
burying dead seeds
they hope the moonlight
will make green again
or cutting out the hearts
of our undisciplined weeds.

Below their calloused knees
well-known and indifferent
worms labor and digest
lost in thoughts of length
and the coiling of links
designed to invade
the very cells of secrets.
As roots explore earth,
grubs assemble and receive
assignments. And while the neighbors
work hunting worms and flowers,
flowers and worms
wait patiently for them.

THE INSTITUTION

Someone, working steadily at night
by dropping water from his canteen,
has worn grooves in the steps
leading to columns pitted as chewed pencils.

The windows are like deep-set eyes;
the door is a leather-bound book no one has read.
A commemorative plaque is worn smooth
as an old coin by many kisses—

just as, inside, the leaders have lost their toes
from wading in the blind reverence
of the people. Terra-cotta statues of them
line the entrance hall; they each have slots

in the top like childrens' banks.
A former hero dozes on a folding chair
chasing the wounded cats of his sleep.
Feet on marble sound like spoons tapping eggs.

Large, furtive insects like pageboys
stare from the shadows and run along
the baseboards. Outside the meeting chamber
a justice of the peace bandages his eyes.

Inside the chamber a school of vagrants
studies leisure or rolls endless cigarettes.
A special subcommittee is in session
planning obscure illnesses for us.

Near the frayed edges of towns,
    the places where roads tire
    of their coats of tar
    and shed them to run bare
    in the dust; there, paired
    lovers roll in the grass
    wrapped in halos of insects,
    wreathed by summers of loneliness.

Out in the country others pretend
    to romp in haylofts,
    mimicking the motions
    of animals, making
    themselves seem robust
    though their bones
    bear the long-planted
    seeds of rickets. Their limbs
    are bowed and thin,
    full of future fractures
    and undiscovered limps.

Elsewhere initials are carved
    in the soft bark
    of sentiment and eternal
    pledges are made.
    Nights are ripe
    with affirmations
    heard through echo chambers.
    And young men scratch

their knees on the pebbles
of their proposals.

Muted, perspiring, the long
nights of adolescence
continue in obscure
parking places where
engagements have been
sealed and bruises found
among cool leatherette.
The marathons of their lives
have come to this:
they hear the parched
runners of their blood
approaching to light
victory fires
in their groins.

And everywhere in rooms
the lamps go down,
the record players play
and parents strain
near sleep to hear
the sounds of zippers,
the tentative noises
of bedrooms, the voices
of couch springs
that accompany
each sugary moan.

From a bench I watch
the grass spread out,
climbing a knoll,
falling into a pool,

looking for the enameled
sheep that are its due.
This lawn is forced
to be green

by the attendant
who coils and uncoils
the drugged snakes
of the hoses, letting them

feed all day
at deep mains.
On the playground
patient children

are learning how
to break the rules
day by day. I see
the cheat, quick hands

making ready
for a future of short
change; the liar
practices his surgery

on the real; and the fool
wears his freckles
like a mask, buckteeth
grinning at the beautiful.

And the outlines appear
here, too, of those
who will always
obey the rules: the informer,

the self-righteous,
leaning into their
peculiar blindness.
Scattered over the field

the graceful and the sure,
those few married
to certainty, score
winning runs and aim

toward disease.
The lovers and the doomed
grow tan, and the good
are somehow learning
the punishing arts
of their losing game.

Up early while everyone sleeps,
I wander through the house,
pondering the eloquence
of vacant furniture, listening
to birdsong peeling
the cover off the day.

I think everyone I know
is sleeping now. Sidewalks
are cool, waiting for
roller skates and wagons.
Skate keys are covered
with dew; bicycles look
broken, abandoned on the lawns—
no balance left in them,
awkward as wounded
animals. I am the last
man and this is my
last day; I can't think
of anything to do. Somewhere
over my shoulder a jet
explores a crease
in the cloudy sky;
I sit on the porch
waiting for things to happen.

O fat god of Sunday
and chocolate bars, watcher
over picnics and visits to the zoo,
will anyone wake up today?

Night settles like a damp cloth
over the houses. The houses that are shut,
that show no wear. Lawns
are patrolled by plywood flamingoes
or shrubbery clipped from magazines.

Nightlocks have been put to work,
their single fists tight in the wood.
Within, each floor has been swept
until bone shines through. Each light bulb
has been washed and polished.

And now the readers of newspapers,
those who savor the taste of box scores,
recline in chairs that have perfect postures.
Air ruffles dry ferns on mantels
and touches intricate clocks beneath bell jars.

A pipe is tamped with a lacquered hand.
Repose flutters in match flare and a face
is turned toward a window. Then, as if seeing
eyes pressed like stamps to the glass,
it turns quickly and lunches on want ads.

Others recline, the army of competence,
the many firm turners of lathes,
the knowledgeable numbers who know
the secrets of fuse boxes, the tricks
of storm windows, the precision with which

flagstones must indent the grass.
They lean back, these artists of roasts,
these heads of tables, listening
to dishes shift in warm water,
hearing bills collect on their doorsteps

like gypsies. Night drops firmly.
Now the second car sleeps beside the first.
The committee meetings are over
and each chairwoman prepares late snacks
of corsages and pewter door prizes.

Some turners of lathes move
toward dreams where they wear
masks with great cleft chins.
Some wives watch their phones grin
at their unused appointment pads.

Others think of daughters driven
to seek, late at night, hot solace
on leather couches; or of sons, failures
as halfbacks, forced to mold cars
around power poles. But they move

toward sleep letting dreams float
as in the tips of fingers. But some
lie awake, chairwomen and handymen,
with thought welded to a single
nipple of light, the glow of a cigarette.

For them the next day treads heavily
in each tick of the clock and they lie
with thoughts moving from the frail glow
inward into a mesh of wires, a fusion
of days and dates, bank accounts

or formal dances years before.
Memories shift scraping along
the tender mind. They remember
those cuts that will not heal,
those growths they cannot explain,

those slights that at the time
seemed meaningless and now grow cancerous.
Some stare steadily into blackness
afraid that they are blind, testing
their blindness. Some listen

to the burglar sounds of their sleeping
houses. Dawn lies coiled in clocks.
There are no conclusions. The dark is there.
Cigarettes burn down and are ground out
in souvenir ashtrays from vacations by the sea.

MIDNIGHT
for Joan

Twelve sprawls on the night
with sharp noises and long silence.
Lights have clicked off
in imitation of all neighbors.
Dust ghosts slide under doors
and settle on shiny tables to accuse
dull housewives on dull mornings.

Stars stretch beyond windows
in the yawning sky. (Midnight is distance
and the sounds of sleeping fathers
that hum through the trees
and over houses.) Our watches tell the hour
that stays all night around limp children
drowned in sleep. Then silence
is chipped by a confused rooster
that crows at the quick daylight
of a passing car, and then forgets this day
like all those that have forgotten
his spurs and bright feathers.

The stars switch on and off
like eyes startled by the sight of earth.
(Our beds revolve slowly
around the moon and prowl the flat night
looking for morning.)

These are the addicts of charts,
the anxious who wait for crises
and side effects, their eyes geared
to read only the scrawls of doctors.
They sit in their lawn chairs
at late evening, hoping the voices
from the high grass will stop,
that they will someday hold
a mower in their hands again
and never sit undressed while doctors
thump their chests like melons.
Something will happen, they know.
The latest abscess applying for admission
to their flesh will prove a fraud;
their x-rays will turn out to be
those of someone else; and they
will be made to lose their appetite
for the fumes of motors in locked garages.
But the voices go on, calling them
to join the dark burrowers, the faint
turners of soil, on vacant lots
where only the dismembered
or decaying are discovered.
But they always save their shining
trump for late evening's final
desolation: They say all weakness
finds its compensation—the blind
hear the steps of ants, the deaf read
whispers and the incurable never die.

THE NEW HOUSE

This place is not ours:
The window sill refuses
to wear our drying wishbone
and the floors don't fit

the worn spot for carpets
we seem to take
everywhere we go.
The house still sings

its own tune, sending
our footsteps along the floor
through timbers that creak
to keep the basement washer

company, peopling that lair
of webs and laundry
where the furnace lifts
its arms to warm

the rooms. But the rooms
are cold, bent
on remembering
other hands caressing

woodwork with soft cloths
and feet that always
tiptoed. Wallpaper
has memorized

the places where
their pictures hung.
Soon enough, we know,
the rooms will give in.

Our own mice will shatter
cupboards and later
we will sprain our wrists
opening new bills.

But last night
windows threatened
to bring in the storm
and the back door banged

and banged, giving us
a message we could understand,
something menacing and wooden
that spoke, asking us to travel
to the storm's blind, silent eye.

The mind, that slow sea creature,
has again begun its drifting
and I think of the long hallways
wit must follow to find a way
to light: Through deep corridors
of coral, passing waving sea grass
and the eyeless, armored fish.

But today I have lost my place
in all the helpful handbooks.
Thoughts simply float among wrecks
discarded by the surface, and I feel
that art demands better weather,
steadier hands than I discover
strapped to my wrists today.

The happy poets always find
some thing—pressed flowers,
a plaster bust—that is water-
tight and holds the powders
of their sense; but in this room
all objects are sieves
wearing the fingerprints

and bent corners of use.
None will hold the meanings
of lives run aground at night—
of hulls foundered in stairwells
containing soaked and spoiled cargo.
I think of the bald eloquence
events all have that words must steal.

I walk around the room,
stop at the frosted windows
and draw on them: A bleeding
valentine, a hanged man—
works of art for such a winter—
and long for coves where thought
may swim but is never forced to dive.

A DAY IN MARCH
for Joan and Matthew

I awoke that day to the usual
weakness of morning: My senses
random as broken beads.
        The day before

Spring had been near:
Buds inched along paralytic twigs,
near waking, numb rumors
        that promised birth.

But that morning the buds
were gone, muffled by sudden snow
spilled over them by midnight.
        Yet birth was going on,

we knew, straining steadily
beneath those white sheets
and today we would count
        the intervals

between each spasm.
And it seemed to us
that to mark the day the world
        had slowed,

shuddered to a halt and brought
out its regal beasts, the lumbering
and lowing snowplows, to parade
      in honor of the event.

For several were trying to be born
that day: A child and a mother
and a father who would find
      their names the moment

new lungs protested the bite
of air. Snow remained,
resisting the blandishments
      of the sun;

day and night passed
and while each of you wrestled
with the problem of being born
      I sat rubbing out

cold thoughts read into my brain
by tales of broken births.
Outside, streets were clearing.
      Salt and sand

had chewed the snow to grit
and the long winter ended
when spring rode in
      on a cry.

THE FAT MAN

I call everyone
shriveled. Dried apples
fit for cellars,
nothing more.
They have no folds,
no flesh to touch—
gangling reminders
of the grave.

Existence melts
in my mouth.
I relish, I taste
the sweet jams of life;
I gorge and worship
the place of love:
All kitchens everywhere.

Diet is sin:
An effort
to turn limbs
to razors that slice
a lover's hands.
Right angles
pierce my eye;
I love the arc,
soft ovals, the curve—
things molded
to be touched,
the soothers of sight.

I feel at least
ten souls
swimming in my flesh.
I feed them
with both hands.
Someday
I will become
a mountain.
I eat the world.

STATEMENT FROM AN APARTMENT

The pictures on our walls
are never seen.
No one marks shifts
in the tones of our voices

or sees our small gestures
of remorse and loss
in exclamations over
the episode of the broken

dish. No one hears the elegies
of our footsteps move to where
we formally mourn the death
of days with toothbrush

and mouthwash.
No guerrillas hide
in the hills of our paintings,
lethal silence falling

from their garrotes.
We have placed blindfolds
on all the keyholes
and gouged the ears

and eyes of the world
which wants, we hear,
to send warrants for us
to join all others

on some drill field
of the passions.
But our wars are here—
with the tripping rug,

the acute gods
of solitaire
or the seated one
across from us.

Our accomplishments
are of chairs.
The blankets about our knees
are flecked with snow

that never melts,
that is not real snow.
Our heroes are the mailman
or paperboy—those

who fight the sidewalks
in all weathers.
Our only real enemy
is the prowler, uninvited,

who wants to wound
our chairs or break
the seals on our roofs
and let the wilting sunlight in.

THE SPARE ROOM

You lie awake. The attic
begins its nightly act.
Moths stir, going through
old pockets; rafters strain
still thinking themselves
the fine bones in wings,
the shingles feathers.

It is taking you to sleep,
to the place of old pictures
and clothes you have
outgrown. In the dark
the clock face shines.
You angle backward into
time. This is the room

of childhood where your
sleeping body counted bruises
all night long as warm
shadows moved above you,
comfort in their hands,
and walked into the premises
of your dream. They are gone now.

The only place you meet them
is in your sleep. You know
there has been some mistake;
they are out there still, beyond

the edges of your sleep, tiptoeing,
holding the night together until
morning comes. And then it comes.

Today the sun's blades slide
through the worn bamboo blind
and in the store below
people are playing bingo
on the cash register
while I try to haunt my mind
with names like Dachau,
Buchenwald or Hiroshima.

But how do you speak
of such things in any terms today
in a room where the sun
distracts, edited into arrows
by the slats of the blind?
What words will carry terror
in a place where the typewriter
weighs heavy with demands

like a medal made of a millstone?
Where there are books, gaunt
and worn, that refuse to spit
their knowledge even though
you break their bindings?
How are such specters of the private
made public ghosts? Downstairs
people are buying out the store

and here books of words lie
dormant and thoughts corrode
the bland surfaces of paper. Below
they are filling a vacancy
their distended cupboards have
never known, assuring themselves
that if all else fails at least
they won't feel the mice

of hunger at their bellies.
Who can tell them that hunger
lives best in the ripe heart
of abundance? They thrive
on this art of taking.
They have finally lost their
childhoods and become adults
with accounts of their own

to overdraw; they have
their own lives like new toys
that demand destruction.
Meanwhile, they buy meat.
There are enough horrors
to blunt any pen today—
people whirr like flies
in rooms below, workmen

with pneumatic drills repair
the street by digging huge

chunks from your consciousness.
What to say? Keep at it, men,
and then go home and wallow
in your canned goods? The strongest
attention is broken by their drills,
the weakest shattered by the sun.

The century is like a large
animal breathing the odors
of its disease above the town.
How does the mind deal with
this malignant time, these
years that grow fat on death
and slake their thirst for chaos
every decade? Casualties

have been piled so high
the senses will not register
death in numbers. Which
among our rusting instruments
will gauge this time
on such a day when typewriters
chew at our fingers
and women in shorts walk

through the spattered sunlight
showing thighs which promise
that though the world may fall
they may spread and let us
conquer it again? The heavy

industry of hate burns factory
lights all night. Deceit
is nurtured in all the gardens

of diplomacy. And the people
in the store below are starving,
laughing and starving. And the women
on the street wear the thick
ankles of embarrassment;
acne scars the surfaces
of their romance packaged
in magazines about their favorite

movie star who sleeps with them
in dreams. Something tears
at the maps we live on;
something mutters in the spaces
between our walls. Like all towns
this town sports its bullseye
and is mounted on someone's chart
like an insect pierced by a pin.

We do not come to terms.
History is ravenous about us.
The sun is burning to a cinder
outside the blinds. Intricate
pressures are building up
below the earth's fetid rind
and we are forced to follow
this century's crippled path.

THE WINDOW

Outside, I walk across the street—
old, cradling a six-pack with arms of chalk
as bells in towers chip pieces from the night.

I stroll along the staggering sidewalk
and from here, this dated day, this window,
the broken rudder of my mind
drifts among the noises of the street
that is the debris of another, future evening.

The bells chip and pick. I walk on.
My belt strains at the round insistence
of my stomach. My feet,
wearing their awards of broken arches,
recoil from stubborn concrete.
Lamplight bathes my bald head;
shadows fall, sifting in the wrinkles
gathered near my eyes.

I sit. The window accepts the rumors
of the wind. Blind trucks run the roads,
their knuckles cracking as gears shift,
carrying cargoes of wealth to someone else.

Outside, I walk on,
numb flightless bird settled in age,
still shuffling toward the future's nets—

now an empty jar, a burnt-out match.
The soot of years settles relentlessly
as I walk toward some dim bulb
remembering myself now—
how I sat plunging thoughts of a future
into the sponge heart of the street.

At the window I hear a desolate phone
ring across lawns of charcoal;
a screen door opens
giving its harsh reply,
a parrot's feeble squawk,
and the old man's memory climbs the stairs
looking for the vacant place
left for him at my table.

THE ADVENTURER

1.

I think of you, burned black
        by the tropic sun
        you carry like a kite
        above your knapsack,

Your mind's edge rubbed sharp
        by the chips of stone
        that are your eyes,
        while I plow deeper

Every year waiting for that day
        when fields lie completely
        fallow and I've taken root
        so deeply that even envy

Will run thin, watered down
        with some commonplace sap
        of this countryside.
        While your feet barely indent

The sand that litters scenarios,
        I sink in mud. My roots
        are still tendrils, blind
        as worms and afraid of the dark.

2.

I stay here watching my thoughts
       of voyages whiten on the banks
       of the river of mud I navigate;
       they become the imaginary

Silver dollars I throw across.
       (We become heroes as best we can.)
       But then I think of you
       threading trails through

The jungles of your desire
       and my despair. Something
       withers when I think of this.
       You pay no income tax.

All your papers are really forged
       while mine seem false
       only because the State
       lacks subtlety—my ID card

Identifies someone else,
       an approximation of myself,
       not myself. I am
       the document that is forged.

3.

Each night you slam
        through my dreams
        on the Orient Express.
        The best I can do

Is to spread my toast extravagantly
        with butter or scandalize
        my stomach with 3.2 beer.
        Each morning I secure

My head with a necktie,
        emblem of the hate that waits
        in the plump hearts of families
        and shows itself at Christmas,

As you swim the heavy oil
        of the Congo or parachute
        behind the lines of my childhood.
        You always go; I always stay,

Remaining a spy without orders
        or purpose. My tunnels
        of escape are always found;
        my compatriots are all informers.

Your actions comment on my life,
        but you smudge your face
        for maneuvers behind the wrong lines.
        Here the war is endless, the enemy obscure.

LAMENTS

We chew it daily
with limp toast, see it
in spiders of falling
hair, the mirrored eyes

riding the rim
of panic, ready
to give in
at a word from us.

Irony wears thin,
the soup we ladle
from puddles at noon,
the torn umbrella

we fight rain with.
And there were such
grand beginnings—
like a movie sunrise,

moons all full
and orange. Now,
the play within the play;
now, the backwater

game, the small
pond called home;
now, our compatriot,
the silly goose.

We stroll the alley
of losers—here loss
is lost, no gift, no
sign of grace.

Our companions live
in shadow, legless runners,
fumblers, strike-out kings.
The play within the play,

the melodrama
so full of puns
we groan all
night, every night.

With day nearly gone
I begin to move.
Mired in slowness
my heavy feet

shift in the dance
of rocks, the tune
so slow no one
has heard its end.

The shuffle, the dogged
step and I am
in the world, blinking.
Running through me

is the sense
of hooved creatures
trying to tie knots,
their labored efforts

wince in my wrists.
I am a whale,
some huge thumb
groping for its hand,

searching through
my sounds
for a voice
inside my anchored tongue.

I push my weight
into the numb cold
looking for an ever
darker night

where the sun
never asks
the eyes to see
and I may live

by touch and nudge.
My fathers lie
deep in tar pits:
The terrible reptiles—

stegosaurus, diplodocus—
all buried in spite
of their armor, their size,
the spiny backs,
the heads of bone.

Coughs waited
in the nap
of old rugs
and shapes
moved in the cellar
among webs,
in rust painted
down walls
by drainpipes,
hidden with insects
in dry grass
behind the house.
We were all
helpless,
even our tall
fathers, forearms
like animals,
all sentenced
to slip away.
We felt it
in that wind,
icy in August,
temperature falling
to zero inside
us. We heard it
in the worn voice
of the couch,
the noises

of other roomers,
the ominous
landlady only
a sound
of pots and pans
on the other
side of the wall.
The war went on
in backyard grass,
the enemy
in our knuckles
winding our lives
up on a spool,
pulling us tighter
toward the darkness
of backrooms,
the standing water
in ditches, last
year's weeds
stiff and pale.
We lay at night,
tied to our
beds, the dark just
beyond our faces
solid—the side
of a huge
fish, a tree
with hands
for leaves, grinning
faces bunched

together like marbles
in a sack.
Floors were haunted
too, and alone
we put wood
chips on each
threshold and listened
for footsteps
on the porch.
Everywhere we
walked we felt
the dead stir
below: Faces from
old pictures, dogs
in shallow graves.
It was plain:
Some hammer
of light would
pound each of us
into darkness
like a nail.
Everyone would go
into the gloom
behind screendoors
in summer,
the dark falling
over all of us
like an old blanket
smelling of mildew
and urine.

BEING AWAY

Changed by distance
the shapes of old friends appear—
rectangular,
stamped with wavy kisses,

ghost-money brought by the man in gray.
The haunt,
they call me back
with words

like tiny hooks.
Each phrase is the noose that waits
at the end of a leash.
I am tripped and snared

by the loops of g's and y's.
But it makes no difference.
I am here. Away.
Forgetting those faces.

Spending whole evenings
erasing a nose or a chin,
moving my mind back and forth
slowly

with the care of a forger
until nothing is left
but a blur, thumbprints
where their faces were.

This is best.
The fine art of forgetfulness
is best—
to drift without memory

through a deep winter
lonely as a man
in a coma, free
as a sleeping bear.

WATCHING

They appear every day from
unseen rooms, born suddenly
behind counters, across aisles, waiting
on corners for buses to drive us mad.

We see them perched in feathers
on little chairs in bars, clipped to menus
in restaurants. We watch, never missing
a movement, studying hard, our eyes

like suction cups, hands squeezing
all those moon thighs, glances walking
like snails over the secret breasts,
prospectors searching for ravines

and rich outcroppings, the vulnerable
willing terrain. Each heel tap
beats in our bellies, the curve
of a cheek loosens elastic in our knees,

old songs scratch our throats as we eat
with our eyes. They stand still
or pass by like cars, sealed in coffins
of self-concern, hors d'oeurvres, billboards,

whispered invitations, always bound
for places beyond any street we know,
freezing us with the rays of a single look
before they dissolve through doors like safes.

Graceful horsemen
of our lives we
explore balance,
the either/or in our
bloodstream, the light
the dark. We
take chances, risk
Park Place
and Boardwalk,
sacrifice pawn
after pawn and ride
roughshod over
each bipartisan hour.
Indeed, we're big spenders
but our real talent
is to overlook, miss
clues, watch
doubt curdling
surfaces as boards
quiver with
agonies of choice
and dice wink
snake-eyes.
All this to feed
our merciless boredom,
this abyss
of the unplanned—time
cannot stand
so still!—but who

the hell said
it was just a game?
We're sure the one
today was called
The Real Thing.
But which one tonight?
Which one?

The pool is now
frozen and small—
a bathroom mirror
concealing ammunition
for the war of decay:
Powders and creams,
dyes and tonics.
But nothing much works.
Staring in the glass
he sees the same worn
version of his lover
and waits hours—petulant,
tapping his foot—for even
a dutiful fondness
to stir his sick heart.

LAMENT FOR MOVIEGOERS
for David

As they say:
It is
a dream.
You walk in
over silent
carpets,
soft nameless music
plays,
you carry popcorn
and a hidden
candy bar—
saving its noisy
unwrapping
until the sound
begins.

As they say:
The houselights
dim
and the mighty figures
come forth.
Scenes change
swiftly—
you make no
effort
as in a dream.

You are passive
and benign
as a sleeping
king.

As they say:
The only pleasure
is to look.
You stare
and your deepest
self
hovers like smoke
in the beam
from the projector.
You swim
without effort.
All things
are accomplished.
All things.
And when you
leave
you are helpless
as a newborn.

Our names burn in the air.
Great reputations descend from the trees
like thousands of caterpillars.
Everyone is famous!

Each house has a marquee!
And no one wears the dark
coat of obscurity
any more. We've thrown away

the sad gloves of failure.
The newspaper is enormous—
all page one, filled with everyone's
picture. The seedy dives

of drift and solace
are closed. No one's name is secret.
Every phone book
is a *Who's Who*

and the movie credits never end—
they list all of us! O never again
will anyone be anonymous and all our graves
will be national shrines!

This is the conclusion
of the season—
flies assail
the horses' asses,
buttocks twitching
and tails awry.
Field trials
are upon us;
the horses nicker
anxiously.
The ladies loll
in their tight jodhpurs
brushing thighs
with riding crops
as, like men,
they fork their horses
ready to ride
their stallions to Hell.
And several Vronskys
eye their Annas
knowing horse blankets
have another use:
Stables have places
in the shadows
not known by clerks
with rabbit ears—
the pale Karenins

who buy the horses
and pay feed bills.
But doom is waiting
at the water hazard;
the Vronskys will ruin
many mares today.
The tightest reins
will weaken and Drive
melt like candles
in August heat.
Revolvers are cocked
and loaded—
nervous safeties
snicker like crickets.
They drift in the air
like plump summer flies
seeking that mare
with a broken ankle
whose misery
they will sting
until that misery
goes away.

1.
All our books used to say
read us   see our fine paper
we have margins and chapters and stanzas
our white space is rich as cream
read us
we have footnotes in italics
and paragraphs
all of different sizes

2.
All our dishes used to say
put your food here
use our sisters the silver
eat from our backs
unused we are nothing
we like to get dirty
to swim in dishpans
to be stroked by the yellow sponge

3.
All our glasses used to say
pour liquid into us
we love the taste of milk or beer
water is sweet   soda   juice
whatever you wish
we like to grow full   then empty slowly
with little beads of moisture on our sides
your touch excites us

4.

All our footstools used to say
though we are only dwarfs
use us
our backs crave your heels
their touch means good luck
always

5.

All our pencils used to say
choose us   we move across paper   we love travel
you can't imagine the multitude of valleys
of mountains and small towns we visit
leaving our black tracks
make lines   drawings   words   we don't care
we see the places only once
but we must see them

6.

All our chairs used to say
put yourself here
empty we are despondent
neither tree nor animal
but when you ride us agitation stops
we dream
we work   we are beasts of burden
we remember the old country
and ancestors
sedan chair   divan   howdah   throne

7.
All our pianos used to say
put your music here
sit down on our bench
press each key over and over
for how else can we sing
then listen to our voices
listen to our beautiful voices

8.
All our doors used to say
open us   close us
twist keys in our locks   shoot bolts
turn knobs all the way around
we can't be hurt
let us swing free of the walls
back and forth   back and forth
ask armies to your houses
so we may swing free

9.
All our mirrors used to say
look into us
otherwise we are lifeless
we need you
we do our best to give fair accountings
we return faces for value received
we are fair
so stare   shave   comb   make faces
whatever you wish
only look   we need you

10.
All our tables used to say
bring your chairs
sit here
we don't mind your elbows
lean forward
put flowers on our backs   and candles
decorate us for feasts
bring hot bowls and platters
to warm us

11.
All our fireplaces used to say
feed us wood and we'll make fire
sit before us
sleep
our andirons are strong
they wince at nothing
they hold up the wood
until it becomes ashes
they never cry out
feed us wood
let our chimneys taste smoke

12.
All our clocks used to say
pay no attention to us
we are obsessed with time
so it passes
we ask only to be wound
so we never miss a second
pay no attention

13.

All our windows used to say
look outside
look outside
lift our blinds
we like the way sunlight
stabs through us
we are pleased with the way
we stay cold all day

14.

All our corners and cupboards and darkplaces
        used to say
come by sometime
see our fine shadows
look into us
and dream
send us spiders and dust
think nothing of us

15.

All our beds used to say
lie down
lie down
it is time for sleep and love
lie down

THE JOURNEY BEGINS

Driven like a fugitive through splintered shadows
I searched all night
for my old houses—
for the other life, the buried one, the lost vanished life.

Where did it live? What was its address?

I worked my way down cold alleys
numbly as an old man threading a needle;
I crossed at the dangerous corners
and passed empty schoolyards
guarded by cyclone fences,
a drone behind slate windows.

Once we dreamed and woke to another dream:
Fishflutter of leaves, sun throbbing dust awake,
the warm stone's shape invented by our fingers.

I entered a door and my hand remembered
a loose bolt, my foot nudged a cracked tile alive
and slid familiar as a broom over the worn threshold.
Again I met the mysteries of cupboards, the prim necks
        of faucets,
the frozen mirror thawed for me.

Upstairs I saw a ceiling light with its knotted string
          like a spider.
I saw the bed and heard the music of its springs again.
Once touched each object shivered.
They pulsed with my old life, these blind witnesses.

Walking alone on a strange street
I feel an old excitement,
a stirring like those car trips
in childhood that promised
another life, a new school
of echoes, the dull cargo
of the fool thrown overboard
for good: An old car climbs
the grade on Cabbage Hill
coughing steam, tires tender
as balloons. I remember
the knocking motor and all
around me the great silence
of held breath before we
breathed the icy summit's view.
The freight of memory
lumbers with me now down
all that twisting altitude.
My cardboard house folds up.
I am on the path again
that shows you how to lose.
Ozone's lost taste on the air,
no wind, no stir in the leaves
fears become eyes, an eye
for each weeping knothole,
eyes on my skin like kisses.
Once there were rumors

of dead grandfathers—muffled
voices in another room—
and whispers of others lost
in the woods, smothered bones
turned to twigs overnight.
I felt the force of the woods—
ferns winked starvation's eyes
and the cougar of the dark
padded close, huge yet so
delicate no twig broke.
The cat is always there
in the forest thick as sleep
near the path that leads
to cold kitchens. Deeper still
I remember the dirt road that led
to the old farm and how the car
bucked and rattled like a milktruck
over potholes, the farmhouse
rising and falling, pines dancing
the sky jagged. I waited
for the plank bridge. It seemed
only an armload of kindling
thrown over the ditch deep
with brown water, boards warped
and split and thin as lath to
let us drown. But I knew
that if we fell it would be
farther, not just into brown water,
but farther, deeper, darker,
colder than water.

We are captives now, prisoners of this
sad air, these terrible rugs,
these chairs that caress and hold,
these surfaces chosen like a new
skin. It's sea level for us from now on.
Here we practice the cottage
industry of the banal; here we
probe the mysteries of the commonplace.
The work is steady, the pay poor.
But we move that way—bloodhounds
of memory, detectives of the ordinary,
explorers in seclusion. And something
always turns up, something to savor
on long winter nights—the ins
and outs of rumor, the intricate creases
of gossip that hint at some vast
answer if we could only find
the key. It keeps us busy chewing
until all the taste is gone
and it takes our minds off our
troubles too: We know the shadows
near us are alive, we know we're
prey. It's calm but we know
the night is armed. And true,
we live in the house of error,
but we live, you see. There are
regions here no map will ever mention;
there are legends, epics on the heads

of pins. Of course teeth grate
in closets and certainly cold hands
reach to us from drawers.
That's only the domestic gothic—
you have it too, a side-issue.
We're after bigger game. It responds
to nothing but our stillness.

Darkness let go of hills
then turned to mist
and snow dust on those
great humped backs
that brood over Indian
graves and secret springs.

You walked the other
way on sentences like
planks, exploring faces,
the life below surfaces.
And behind all that was
what you now have—

the evening. You look
at dandelions, heads
gray fuzz, and pick
them with watchmakers'
hands only to blow
them away, calling it

confetti for some future
small victory. But
it won't work. Somewhere
during the day you
were beaten, duped,
enrolled in madness;

but there are no signs—
only the spirit of a bruise
around you like smoke,
the ache of the flu
just before it happens,
thoughts like gnats,

nothing will settle.
It was speaking
and not speaking.
That and the razor
edges of hours
and cups, all those

calm minutes. Now
the voices of happiness
whisper, telling you
secrets about yourself
you did not know
and cannot believe.

The house is crowded
as a nightmare
and there are places
to go. You go to
those places. You
come back again.

Thought darts inward like a tongue
and tastes the pale atmosphere
of the past. But it's like a dream.
The faces have no features.
The rooms are all unfurnished.
We live in daylight now
and travel by standing still,
history coiled in the local, in data
our eyes gather at a window,
not in letters stamped strange
with time and distance
sent from a lost world.
In a stranger's house we feel
the burglar's thrill, the special
pleasure of the trespasser
stepping lightly on forbidden
ground. Only our faces swim
the surfaces of mirrors
and there are no ghosts
for us, no footsteps,
no Other fumbling locks or foraging
the midnight kitchen. Late at night
we prowl at will. We run
our hands over anything we choose.
We read all their books like thieves!

OTHER LIVES

You see them from train windows
in little towns, in those solitary lights
all across Nebraska, in the mysteries
of backyards outside cities—

a single face looking up,
blurred and still as a photograph.
They come to life quickly
in gas stations, overheard in diners,

loom and dwindle, families
from dreams like memories too
far back to hold. Driving by
you go out to all those strange

rooms, all those drawn shades,
those huddled taverns on the highway,
cars nosed-in so close they seem
to touch. And they always snap shut,

fall into the past forever, vast lives
over in an instant. You feed
on this shortness, this mystery
of nearness and regret—such lives

so brief you seem immortal;
and you feed, too, on that old hope—
dim as a half-remembered
phone number—that somewhere

people are as you were always
told they were—people who swim
in certainty, who believe, who age
with precision, growing gray like

actors in a high school play.

THIRST

It comes and goes.
We live with ourselves
for hours every day
and night twists

in our minds—
corkscrew of memory,
our throats dusty
as old playgrounds.

We wait for summer
showers—that smell
of rain-dampened
dust, dryness and wetness

mixed, unheard of
marriages. We have
the dryness, our
partner; we go

fifty-fifty, democratic
for days at a time,
listening to old
stories of ourselves—

back in those great
times when raisins
were grapes. And very
late now the ancient

camels gather on
the lawn, filling
darkness with
laments. They

regret their choice
of occupation,
hate their stupid
humps and want

us—for just
one hour—to
turn them into
fish. We try.

JANUARY THAW

In the mud we
begin to understand.
Fictions fall away—
old skin, old hair,

old midnight pledges
scale in wet light.
Whatever was following
has caught up.

It is with us now.
Old vacancy, old tramp
riding the train
whistles, old ugly

come to visit,
old bastard Daddy
crazy drunk, warbling
hello and hacking

like a bullfrog.
We are his favorites.
His dark pockets
are stuffed with gifts—

Christmas candy matted
with lint and tobacco
is peeled out like ore
and it is just for us.

All day the frantic
mill shouted
wooden tallness
down: Every
tree shall be
a conscript
to the cause
of paper!
But now the slow
rumor of a tug
slides by;
log rafts
huddle in dozing
schools
nibbling shore;
a lone canoe
cuts the surface
like a paperknife
scattering moonlight;
and downstream
the Ferris wheel
in the park slowly
mills the night.

THE HOUSE AT NIGHT

Everyone has gone away, buried
in dreams. It is still. The house
is mine. I let go and fill
the space, moving at first
with the stealth of dust, then
rolling from corner to corner like surf,
inhabiting each square foot,
furnishing all the rooms. The house
is packed, pumped up like
a tire, even the dead air
near the ceiling is mine as I
expand, become a king, a whale,
the royal dragon of possession.
Finally, I am the house, tasting
the wood's swirled grain
in my veins and feeling nails
bite where the blueprint said *yes*.

He walks late at night among the enamel ghosts of the
      kitchen—
white blur of the stove, the tall refrigerator like the spirit
      of defensive tackles—
and adds coffee to his cup, feeding wakefulness.
Caffein tightens nerves and he settles in the big chair,
its arms familiar as his own, worn places and stains he has
      made
like moles seen in the shaving mirror each morning.
The forms of his family move around him in a single shape,
a geometry he can never decipher, some pentagram of the
      senses.
They sleep. He stays awake, a sentry against invasions by
      darkness.
Registers knock. Vague shapes demand entrance. Stillness
      quivers between each sound.
His ears ready themselves to hear moans and screams down
      the street.

Guarding over the strangers in himself hatched by the late
      hour,
he senses the push of feelings he thought were lost,
memories sent forward like cryptic communiques
from overrun outposts of the past. The wind jimmies
      windows.
He listens hard to the seashell sound of quiet.
The house whispers to the trees, its cousins.

94 Upstairs, his children float, youth bed and cribs like rafts,
and he sees himself below that surface
where faceless creatures swim, their eyes antennae,
their atmosphere thick and heavy as grease.
They say nothing to him. His name is their food.
Tenderness rides out in filaments toward those rafts.
Then the quick weakening of love and fear hits.
Helplessness comes over him like a disease.
The fists he must have dissolve into limp hands, bones like
        paste.
He knows again how days are measured by injury.

This point, this early hour, is a peninsula he has driven to,
the farthest distance from demands—a delta fear deposits.
Here he must learn to bear his name while remaining the
        boy in snapshots,
thinly disguised in the heavy body he now wears.
And now he understands the men who turn errands into
        getaways,
flying off for good on a loaf of bread.
Like seeing a crack of light in absolute dark
he even understands those who stay and kill each person
        near them.
He understands. The shotgun blast is their only music;
the antidote to their disease is death, divided equally;
the geometry of the family cancelled all at once,
those limbs connected by the thinnest strands severed too,
a shape grown too large to carry in the mind, shattered.
He shudders with the sashes, shaking his head quickly,
        moving thoughts away,
disordering those puzzle pieces to begin again.

Somehow he must find safety from cold, night terrors,
the stilettos of chance, the heaped refuse of lies
at the curb of each day. But protection is most dangerous,
     he knows—
to defend we occupy and destroy.
The tendons in his wrist slacken, cut by need.
The great weight of the world pulls from his grip.
He sees it avalanche down, hurtling in the dark
toward the lives surrounding his, defenseless in sleep.
Or do they sleep? Standing, he goes upstairs to pause beside
     his wife,
to lean over the sleeping children listening to their breath,
riding it like a feather. He bends and touches them,
pushes at blankets, strokes their heads, knowing he must
     . live
by touching, that his name and the names of those he
     touches are never known—
no language stretches that far. They live. They still live.
He undresses in the dark and lies down with his wife
and begins floating through darkness to the shallow glassy
     light of morning.

No one tells you how it's done—
you are expected to know—
to, say, be able to get up every day
at an hour when rising is like pulling gauze from a
        wounded eye,
and then laugh, scratch, greedily eat eggs
without ever mentioning those sad lakes, the yolks.
Worse, it's assumed you know who you are right away
and have a name printed on the tip of your tongue, ready.

The fools go on complaining of infinite illnesses,
mapping your mornings with routes of disease,
filling the air with lamentations and the woes of bunions
        or hangnails
and you're expected to take all this equably,
to nod even though the fools go on living, steady as
        drumbeats,
while the brave are beaten up and the good die like a
        snap of the fingers.
No one mentions this and if you so much as write secretly
on the back of a stamp, "Fools are fools"
you're thrown in jail and told this is your democratic
        privilege.
It's sacred—like the liquor commission or the Bureau
        of Love
where you get dog licenses and snakebite serum.
But no one tells you how.

You're expected to fall in step on the street
and reserve your deepest emotions, your tenderest
        sympathies,
for mannequins without even the suggestion of nipples
        or pubic hair.
And from the beginning words surround you:
Glucose, semester, artichoke—they make no sense—
and you're supposed to like the morning paper
with its printed directions for suicide
that tells you the Pessimist Party is plotting mortality.
No one tells you how.

Others expect you to know what to do at all times
and not simply wander around eating plums
or watching fog in the trees.
They expect you to work and, as they say, work
        honorably all morning
and then stop precisely at noon,
forget the vast complicated ritual of work,
eat again, laugh and talk about weather
even if none exists.
And then just as you begin to develop a taste for
        this indolence
you're sent back to work that might even be dangerous.
And this is expected when some, like you and me,
may find it hard mastering the art of walking up stairs
or spend hours trying to recall our birthstones
or the names of people we're told we love.

And this is only the beginning.

98

Days come fast.
And you must remember dental appointments
and the size of your hat.
They laugh and prepare cells for example
if you forget and go to work on Sunday;
and there are whispers behind your back
if you call Wednesday a pet name, say, Carburetor.
And if you ask questions so much the worse.
You're lost if you say: Why do you punish your doors
        with locks?
How do you know they like the flavor of your
        keys?
Or, how many times does a stranger
squeeze your doorknob with a passion
to sit on your chairs so hard they wear out?
Or, does someone want to drink all the water
        from your taps?

You begin to learn
how it's done
when it's too late:
and at night
if you fall
out of bed
no one cares—
and you even have to teach yourself
the proper technique.

You are the secret conscience of the age.
Your power is confirmed
in the milkman's punctuality.
And likewise the paperboy
honors you with paper.
Every day such events
argue the fine print
of your significance
and this says nothing of the seasons—
the way they change—
or the tides or the snow on mountains.
They all pay homage to your majesty.
Indirection is the method—
your name kept secret
for the sake of
Anarctica's integrity
and the sacred ovoid of the egg.
Thus your obscurity legislates.
Everyone reads the volumes of your silence.
Everyone studies your omissions.
Yet you neglect nothing, you take responsibility
for it all; you have high principles
and a strong sense of duty.
Without you the signature of all things
would be illegible. Without you
box-scores would lie
and the seas run dry.

You see this everywhere, these examples
of your strength—the moon
your baseball, the law of gravity
your invention. The mailman's daily passage
says so, the rising sun
affirms it. All bow down, all sing praises
with their actions—
bartender and shoe clerk, the voice
that gives the time on telephones.
All obey.
You are the secret law that all revere,
alpha and omega,
the force that causes runs·in stockings,
the absentee landlord of the dust,
the keeper of bees and brothers.
All kowtow.
All sing your praises—
the wetness of rain, the heat of summer,
the blackness of coffee,
the eyes of needles,
the spokes of wheels,
the links of chains.
You see the signs
and are comforted.
The attendant who sells you gas
shows deference.
The grocery clerk speaks softly.
Your breakfast spoon reflects
your face. Your bed

is always ready.

Your omniscience is astounding.
Your key turns and the door opens—
a sign!
Your coins fit slots
in cigarette machines—
a sign!
Signs! Signs! Everything you touch
answers you.
The movie usher calls you "Sir"!

On the porch I smoke
    and watch cars go by—
    few at this hour—
    hitching rides
    in my thoughts
    to any destination.

There is a door somewhere
    that won't ripen
    until my knuckles rap
    and it falls open
    like a blossom.
    But there is no map
    for such a trip—
    only clocks and calendars
    suggest a way: Wait,
    listen, grow old.

The night is so still
    no pistol shot
    could waken it.
    I lean back, tagging
    a white convertible,
    wondering where I might
    wake up tomorrow,
    what new life
    I could be planted in
    like a bullet
    buried in a tree.

My thoughts chase
      that white car until
      I stand on a vacant lot
      feeling the tough thrust
      of each grass blade
      and a network of roots
      finer than hair.
      I sense hunger in that field
      dry as lint as I look
      at an old foundation—
      a few boards, nails
      only rust stains—
      and slowly rebuild
      the house and enter
      quietly as an old dog
      with the newspaper.

I live in those rooms.
      Children grow. Old people die.
      Chairs and tables shudder,
      wearing out. I see a place
      near the sink where the floor sags
      and a spot on a window
      someone wore thin with staring
      waiting for me to appear.

Now they are loading the old Ford in the evening, taking
     too much luggage,
too much fried chicken in paper sacks, lost
even before leaving the muddy driveway.
With great care they jammed dirty shirts and underwear in
     the cracked suitcase,
everyone's clothes together, rank and wrinkled, the flanks
of the case already sprung, the lock losing its hold slowly.
Cardboard cartons filled with rusty towels, a half box of
     cereal,
the iron with the frayed cord go into the back seat
with army blankets and the squat thermos, spout dripping.

The old man sits very still on a kitchen chair while the
     women work.
His wife, near seventy, sighs and trembles
afraid of highway curves—blowouts hover on the road,
some vast clock figures collisions, fiery breakdowns coil
under the old car's hood. All afternoon she
travelled that long highway, conjuring each dangerous inch,
seeing guardrails spring open like gates
and the flimsy car soar and bounce down ravines
so deep no one has seen the bottom.

The old couple know only that their fat daughter has come
to rescue them from his sickness, its confusion, its haze
around them like woodsmoke.
She drove five-hundred miles fueled by her mother's
        hysteria:
He was dying but still stumbled into town to drink,
swollen hands like mittens around a shot glass.
Drunk, he beat those big hands blue on the woodshed door.
Sober, he said the bar was there to keep him
from sitting like some old woman eating toothless bread
        and milk
with a baby's spoon hooked around his thumb.
He staggered home by moonlight, screaming through
        jackpine
for Bud and Ed, both dead twenty years,
to wake up and have a goddamn drink.
So his daughter—forty-five, three hundred pounds—
drove all night, losing count of flats,
splashing water into steam on the radiator.
Even now as they load the car she eats leftovers.
Her hands always seem greasy, the skin around her mouth
        glistens
and her lips shine as if she had just licked them
before having a picture taken.
You were always such a pretty girl, her mother says. So
        pretty.

The car sags with its burdens, mud high on the fenders like
a watermark,
one headlight squinting blindly through the gloom.
The suitcase is now loosely tied on the trunk with
        clothesline—
the daughter counting more on balance than tension
in the line to hold it there. It is her way.
Springs lurch as they get in, the old man settling his
        brittleness
among blankets and boxes in the back.
Now fear of the road becomes worry over the house:
For the old woman every shingle becomes tinder,
every rafter flammable as balsa wood.

They set out in the dark along a dirt road, a blizzard
        of dust
around them from a passing logging truck.
Soon the old man sleeps.
His daughter counts his breaths in the rearview
        mirror.
The old woman winces at every branch that
        looms swiftly
like an enormous hawk above the car,
scrapes and thumps a claw once and is gone.
The car creeps and whines until they reach the
        cool blacktop,

suddenly free as skaters on the interstate.
But the wrong turn has waited patiently all day
and they take it gracefully, relaxing on the level road.
The old woman even hums and forgets fire.

They drive on, their lone map lost in a sack of
       fried chicken,
grease spots forming on it slowly, darkening the land.
Chainsmoking and swearing the daughter keeps
       steering north,
trying somehow to lean her bulk toward the West,
but the road refuses and they go on and on
as the dark smothers the car
and the blazing white hospital sheets recede
       with each
wheezing mile the old man breathes away.

DRINKING LATE

The others have gone, the last voice
clipped in two by the nightlock,
the final laugh choked silent
by the storm door's click.
I study my glass for secret meanings.
The night's sad music settles
and I swim among my own
sweet dregs, flying the flag of myself
over another dead party.
The dying fire still conjures
a few images: The dead year, parted
friends, assassins and saboteurs, lovers
unknown and unknowable.
Embarrassment troubles us more
than cruelty—I laugh and wince at once
sorting my own collection of gaffes,
my year's supply. We're kept awake
by our fool's cap and bells
rattling the round hours hollow.

My thoughts dance on hurt feet
and I take another drink
letting it study me all the way down,
letting it make the easy journey
that puts the nerves to bed

singing fear its nonsense lullaby.
It's time for the pale life, the life
without desire, the life of the invisible.
But there is the damned year to go over—
skimmed, not read with care of course.
Twelve months of error recorded
in ink, each slip of the tongue notarized,
the few windfalls already bronzed
and lost in the toybox. Those Mondays
like burned forests, weeks in the stocks
of a chair, days of stumps and rubble.
But there was also that vision, slim
goldfish, animal grace and spirit
linked, wish and gesture the same
flesh, the sea writing our names with water.

From my sea-view window I wave
December down, wave at presumed beacons
and phantom ships, wave the way
a soldier shipping out might wave
in a bad movie. But no one's there,
only the breakers' dull lather.
I doctor the scene with a little
more bourbon. Party over, bottles emptied
and ashtrays filled with the usual
casual skill, now it's time to invent:
A crowd just outside. I throw open
the window. Faces look up anxiously,

cheeks like porcelain with tears
of adoration. But I am the Pope of Silence
and merely wave—blessing enough
for such lack of restraint. Faces crumble
and flutter away like discarded leaflets,
the beach empty as the aftermath
of another demonstration of impotence.

The party is down to the hard core—
me. *Neskowin, Ecola, Hebo*—I roll
local names on my tongue like pebbles.
California rides up the coast passing
out cigars and wooden nickels.
Neahkahnie. Rockpools harbor
hearsay galleons, doubloons of coral
and bottlecaps. Old fevers crawl, singing
poverty and dollars, summers made
to order, gift shops decked out like
junior proms. But whatever happens
the Pacific still yanks the coastline
in place like a bedspread. There is
delight in this, history swallowed
like an oyster. And then it all returns
to the private, the bleak assertions
of middle-age: Giving up cigarettes,
rich foods—denial. We attack the senses
with denial to show our passion.

Our hearts whittled to the size of walnuts!
Yet with an athlete's skill we pour our
feeling in the dark and practice sympathy
by candlelight. Guilt is brought out like
old silver to start the abject parade,
abasement done with impeccable taste.
It shows one's humanity, everyone saying,
"Look how open and honest he is."
I see the dead evening this way, how so
many spin out the sticky nets of their
compassion. But the mesh is wide
and they settle for interior design,
the Byzantine ulcer. Night is now
the skin of a balloon against
the windows but I wave to my crowd
anyway. They are happy. Their team has won.
Their shoulders are notched for heroes,
their hands are paddles designed only for applause.
I close the window and open the bottle.

Taste-buds have memories: Afternoon's flint,
the vacancy of three o'clock, the absolute
zero of the world—no wind, only the stir
of old papers, old men with stucco skin,
sex a frown and indigestion—all such
beautiful things drove us inside Monday
after Monday, drove us into cool taverns,

clipjoints, clubs, dives, roadhouses where
we danced on little round tables, on sawdust,
on linoleum, on oiled floors in the mountains
where moose heads stared down
indignantly and mounted fish never blinked.
All night we had the bees of talk,
dragonflies, scorpions fished from glasses,
crickets in the brain while our heroes
for the night fell off their barstools
to cheers and great applause.
I sit back, the dark an envelope, the sea
only a rumor, unconfirmed.

Thought slows, wades through sand
looking for nourishment, windfalls of feeling
nudged to places of honor in the mind.
It's that time of the morning, nursed
into being with care. Now, for a time
the world repairs itself, all cracks healed,
all doom swabbed antiseptic, scars
wiped away like smudges. Worry snores
deeply, stupidity is papered-over with
vast diplomas of intelligence, the mind
like a dart, like a swan, like an eagle's
eye. But then from trying too hard
this passes. Sharks of disorder surface
in the blood, the radio plants
hairline fractures in the skull and I

only want exile—like the poets of China
during 'The Years of Darkness.'
Li Po, this is a night of darkness. If I
could find it I would offer the moon
a drink but it's mostly a dartboard now.

They knew the vertigo of nothingness—
life a racehorse glimpsed through a crack.
We cower behind our addresses, we cling
to the rags of our names. They were seized
with grief—tombs overgrown with weeds, moss
by the gate, mirrors too dusty to reflect.
Their hearts, consulted, knew no answer.
There was a way that was no way.
This is familiar enough. I toast your
dust with oblivion. You turned down
the world's bribes—sometimes—
and found beds of straw sufficient.
(Beds of straw and a little spring wine.)
We call it interior exile, secretly pleased
to travel without passports, to travel without
moving. You had your beds of straw. We settle
for nailbeds of metaphor and racks of guilt—
mixing cultures. But we think them
furniture enough. You would understand.

In city after ruined city merchants sold greed
and poverty, duckweed flourished

in the wells, snakes nested on the sacred
altars. Pain and ruin are not exotic
and we taste them twice in images
like this. Floorboards creak menace—
the old music. We become our own shadows.
We live by proxy. Yes, yes
and some nights I am scarcely here.
Some nights I must think hard to find
myself. Some force thinks me away.
Some vagueness erases me and I'm
carried into mists, into clouds without shape
or voice. All my aching bulk, the face
I've learned to wear, my solid citizen's
disguise—all this turns powder, then
less, then fog outside a stranger's house.
Some nights it is like this. But not tonight.
I know my way around this room.

I walk around, not staggering, never slurring
a single thought and discover the odd
beauty of eggs and the unexplained wilderness
beneath a chair. And wonder of wonders—
there's still some bourbon in the bottle,
true money in the bank. And somewhere
even at this butt-end, even in these dregs,
the grave of winter and war, breakers
saw toward shore and gulls lift their heavy
bodies like Indian clubs, shrieking at first light.
Sir Echo, how about a belt? Li Po, just a little taste?

PARAGRAPHS

The knives on the table are there for a purpose, but their true function has been forgotten over the years. Actually, the lunchroom which now appears so calm and civilized is an arena, the trays and tables converted shields, and we who sit so quietly are gladiators. The man who cleans up, the one who looks so dull, grew tired of the mess and has cleverly diverted us by serving food to slice and eat, thereby satisfying our need to use weapons, which he stealthily reduced in size until they now seem innocuous, just as he has assuaged our desire to kill by teaching us the rudiments of gossip.

Not willing to exert the mind enough even to sense the quality of the lives of those nearest us, we will, however, late at night, create from scratch around a few random sounds in the cellar—pipes knocking, the furnace working—a whole human being, the prowler come to punish us for lack of love.

My dancer stands still most of the time—like an anchor. In fact, his feet leave the ground only when he hoists himself into bed. Your dancer may spin and jump. My dancer sneers and says, "I hate sweat!" His background? Close-order drill at Fort Benning, trick knees, poor wind. Here are a few of his dances: The Dance of Spilled Milk and Burned Food; The Morris Chair Polka; The Tango of the Coffee Urn; The Linen Closet Schottische; and, his masterpiece, The Coma Mazurka.

Just now they moaned as they always do. They are in pain when someone presses the button which is for them like the exposed nerve in a bad tooth. So they scream until the pressure stops and allows them to sink back to what they like best: silence, moisture beading on their lips, darkness.

You see a woman you know and, unaccountably, you become embarrassed. You stammer and can't wait to get away. It is only later that you remember: yes, last night you were together—in your dream. The next time you see her you look closely, eagerly seeking some hint of embarrassment in her actions.

Though they seem carefree and childlike, golfers are, in fact, very sinister. Their ease and playfulness is merely a coverup, a very clever one, for their darker aims. You may have noticed that newspapers occasionally print articles telling of people who have been injured or even killed by golf balls. Following such reports you will notice golfers grow restive and self-conscious. They are afraid they will be found out because the whole vast apparatus of golf has been developed to accomplish a single purpose: assassination.

Given their natural inclinations toward betrayal, they cannot be trusted. They introduce foreign elements into our lives; they encourage appetites we exhaust ourselves resisting or satisfying; or they develop their own vices of the cells which we call disease. And since we have only their little hands to work with, we are helpless against them.

No one sees him standing beside the file studying his mail—all flyers, all third class. No one watches him in the lounge where he pretends to read trade journals, pages all blur and flutter. He is lonely this way all day. No one notices him as he eats slowly in the cafeteria, and though he even likes the food no one knows he does. Every day he is like a man wandering through a strange city looking for a place he can afford, but no room is cheap enough.

"Today I fly over roofs. I am a cloud with a purpose, an enormous Chinese kite with the fat cheeks of a fish. All afternoon I table-hop from building to building, chimney to chimney. I come home to each of you who waits so anxiously, to each of you I come back, and tell strange stories until you fall dreamlessly to sleep, finally cared for as you were always meant to be."

"Dear_____:

I carry cigarettes only because you may want one some day and my pockets are filled with matches, too. I sit in taverns for hours because some evening you may come in, decide to be a drunkard and want drinking companions with experience. I left the space at the top of this letter blank, of course, so that you may fill in your name."

We are told the age lacks faith, that no permanent values exist, that the world is unstable, but many, let us call them the heroes of punctuality, who would follow a dogma if it existed, have circumvented the problem by making of their routines, protocols, schedules, and agendas a watertight doctrine which they always adhere to, as they say, religiously.

Nearly everything you see inspires suspicion. Little signals speak of the ominous future the world has in store for you. But this is only the condition of optimum health, indicating that, like a cat, you are wary. Such a state cannot harm you. The harmful thing is not to suspect, but to know.

I sit in the soft chair, or something very like me sits there, smoking and watching. They come in: The creature of effacement, all but invisible; the typographical error who is never corrected; then, a whole flock of shrugs and winces, closer together and more interdependent than bricks. There are eyes, hands, pimples, coffee—each creature like a simple declarative sentence repeated day after day.

There is a great deal to be learned about conduct from this art. First, a decisive thing is done to an unblemished surface, the tool makes a clear deep line, and because of its general similarity to a pencil line the amateur often thinks of the work as a drawing until the print is made. Then he learns that the whole flat untouched surface is really like a pencil, strange and blunt to be sure, and that further, everything has come out backwards.

We write it often—our pens have memorized its contours and lines, our fingers are intimate with the complexities of loops and dots, we know this little drawing better than our wives. Yet when signing a check why are we so nervous? Why do we feel that someone, *The One Who Knows*, will suddenly lean his padded shoulder across the counter menacingly and accuse us of forgery? And why do we know that we will, of course, be found guilty?

WALKING HOME

FROM THE ICEHOUSE

You wake with the taste of lost miles
of driving fast through dark mountains
of hairpin and horseshoe, of altitude
and icy air. Like a mist
sadness rides over. Was it a dream?
Like a mist it enters.
The pores of the house take it in.
You breathe it in like dust. And those figures—
shapes behind glazed windows—
ghosts? bit players from other nights?

This all you have—
hard substance
ground to powder. Everything pulled
from your hands. Your own life too
like ash sucked up the chimney—
the tombs of China, your father's unmarked grave,
dust, dust, you move in strangeness.
You wake to oilcloth and linoleum.
You wake to the blemished mirror.
There is dust on everything. The secret
tops of books, piano keys, dimming
glistening leaves. The sad mist falls
like dew, like tiny grains for each eye.

Every day the same question in your mouth
for answer a sigh.

That great emptiness behind the stars
those huge clouds of cosmic dust
in their slow dance. You search the familiar
the way a man rips open
his wallet like a fish
to find his name.
Nothing, not even hangover, nothing.

You dress in strange garments
their touch soothing your hot skin.
And still that sense of travel, running in the night,
fear. Dust on everything, the house breathes it sighing.
You taste desert. Everything ground to powder.
You drift out to a street you've never seen.
Sunlight burns. You blink hard.
Frame houses, locust whirr
the sound of baseball in the distance.

It feels right. But the dust
keeps falling
dazzling in the sunlight, snowflakes of gold leaf.

You taste the cold desert. The houses shrivel.
Everything ground to powder. The body knows.
Bones pulverized
to make the flour that makes the bread
the giant eats.

They have brought you here
where a fine brown silt
covers everything. You want
to ask about color
but it is too late.
They have taken that away.
You eat your brown food
with your brown spoon
and talk softly
with your dark cousins, their
bony arms starved thinner
by shadow. You see the sadness
they call possessions,
the helpless objects
they brought here with great effort—
old generators, bald tires,
a trunk full of mildew,
slaughtered mountains
of the broken and useless.
Then slowly in the exhausted light
they divide it up
making sure you get your fair share.

I move back by shortcut
and dream. I fly above
it all, the dark stain
where swamps soak up
the lake's extravagance,
stubble hills, the valley's
green finger. This is the place
of pure invention, secret
as old wood
under a hundred coats
of paint. I invent
my own way back, invent
these wings, this
Piper Cub of tissue paper
I glide in, circling the valley
chasing my shadow across
the lake, twisting each layer
back through air.
The town scatters out
along the highway and I cut low
buzzing the school, signaling
my old teacher's chalky bones.
I bank away approaching town
along the old road
that rises from a low plain
where the land tastes bad,

where dust even slips
under rich men's doors.
I trace it like a route
on a map and it climbs
kept company by a creek
with a mouth full of boulders.
I finger wind for updrafts
slowing above the dump,
then sweep around the lake,
past Indian Village
and summer homes,
steering hard I top
the mill, my steering wheel
an old lard can lid
on the end of a stick,
my seat a log set back
in the woods, the shade cool
and safe in the arc cut
by the rope swing
thirty years ago.

I pick a year, say 1932
and travel back by hearsay,
back to the old kitchen
with its glass of spoons
in the exact middle
of the table.
We are there together
letting it all get too much
for us, letting it all build up,
sitting night after night
with only two sounds—
her radio, our steady honing.
The snick and whirr,
the static straight from Boise
and every blade already
keen enough for surgery.
How much coffee can you drink?
How sharp do knives have to be?
It's one of those times
we dread and long for—
the cold bedroom, the single bed,
getting up at five
to work the pond.
(We're like cats on those logs.)
But it's all too much for us.
How much kindling can you chop?

It's one of those clockwork times—
three months gone and time
to get the hell out,
time to trade that whetstone in
on the rusty edge
of bootleg booze.
Think we'll go into town, we say
and get out
just before the skillet hits the door.
Woman's got a hell of an arm, we say.
In town we hear the skillet ring
and let the first drink
slide down slow as summer weather.
That's a little better, we say,
just a leetle better now.
Let the goddamn radio
dim those blades dull again
we don't care. We're here
and by god we'll stay
until we drink our paycheck dry.

In Long Valley the Finns
Brought the old country with them
Brought it in the 'nineties
In steerage in their ragged luggage
They lugged it with them
It was a millstone and the knives in their boots
It was the way they stood around
The store in town
Eyes down shoulders hunched
Waiting for everyone else to buy
They packed it with them in gunny sacks
They took it to dances
Condensed and distilled
In pint bottles
They beat each other with it
Behind Finn Hall
Its weight pulled
Them out of school at fourteen
It ruined their teeth with hardtack
And filled their mouths
With strange accents
No soap would wash loose
It was the broken axle and the bad crop
It was the huge tree
They knew would fall
They smiled grimly

Knowing 1929 by its real name
It let the travelling dentist
Pull all my grandfather's teeth
The year he died
It was in the washrag I buried
For my father
To cure a wart

BUILDING THE HOUSE

Among shadows and pieces,
the scraps of old houses,
I clear a place, tamping earth
flat, and draw a plan
in the dirt. I lean toward
the old house, that long vacancy
and scar where it stood,
that address of absence.
Out of nothingness and shadow
I try to build it up again.
I begin with kindling
and mill ends. I use
the carboard tools of memory.
How was this room? I feel
my way along a floor, fingers
remembering. I try again
to revive each board,
remember it into being
and with effort hold it in mind
until it falls in place beside
the others and the nails slip in
soundless as pins. Under way now
the walls rise, every board
finds its place, each one a word
each wall a page, and the rooms
come back easy as sunrise
revealing each oval picture,
each square of old linoleum.

One by one they add themselves,
darkness brushed away like cobwebs—
the house new and old at once,
fresh nails in blond wood
bleed rust down flaking paint.
Holding it in mind I move
through its lives—sawdust
of newness, sag of neglect,
weeds of abandonment.
It breathes back and forth
as I breathe, my breathing
keeping it alive. I put in
windows and replace the matchstick
rafters. I add shadows
to the corners and scoops of dreams
for each bedroom. Holding my breath
I deliver all the cheap furniture
at once. I put everything
in place like a watch—
my ship in a bottle, memory's toy—
until it's nearly ready, swept
new again and waiting
for its family. Lamplight strokes
the trees alive, smoke dreams
from the chimney. Finally
I add the brass knob,
then enter and meet
the cold music of empty rooms.

VISITING DAY

Dark presence, old crow, hag
face at the window
our wrists are icy with your grip,
our tongues go numb.
Take these flowers, this candy.
We're muffled, your shawl
covers us all, we see
through its weave only—
helpless, tall as we are, helpless
remembering the dark places
you studied into being
inside each of us—lesson after lesson,
detail upon detail. And none
could run far enough.
One fled eating great handfuls
of scripture. She is here, submissive,
a good girl now. Another
took a wife but your icy fingers
held his genitals tight
and small as a baby's.
He is here, too, shy as a boy,
hair combed flat and wet.
Others stayed close, drawn
by your dark fire, and suffered
the twisted kiss of abscess and ache,
haywire age gobbled them

early. Still others you
pumped up with fat—
they ate and ate searching for the food
you never served.
They loll here now, wheezing
nibbling peanuts, eyeing your forbidden candy.
What did you want?
We offered our torn flesh
for patches, we swallowed
every button you offered.
What did you want?
We've allowed our brains
to curl tight as a rat's,
curled like the meat
in a nut, like the core of a golf ball.
What did you want?
It took years—diplomas,
certificates, even prizes—
believe me it took years.
We know the maze.
Was this it, old rip?
We moved in the shallows,
in the school districts
of middle age. We wore
dark suits and combed our hair.
Was this it?
You knit. We're lifted still
with the skein, we feel the needles
in and out, in and out.

But what is enough?
Told to love lies
we loved them. No one
crossed his fingers. No one.
And no one should doubt us.
The lies were lovely—intricate,
of durable materials.
But no one believed us.
We wept—as we weep now
here with these flowers.
To atone we were given small whips
made of our mothers' hair.
Punish yourselves, a voice said, a voice
like yours. Punish yourselves
we have no time.
Our knees were raw with thanks.
We developed the art of the welt.
We favored the baroque—
are you listening?—
we favored the baroque
and scoffed at impressionism.
There were one or two cubists.
They were despised.
Did you see that?
Did you approve? Was it worth
a few cookies? The kind with raisins
we spent our dark childhoods
pretending to like?
This was all for you.

We obeyed ourselves into debt.
We followed rules
until our feet were bloody.
All for you. All for you.
We have done what we can.
The dead bring their bones,
the living their nerves loose
as old clothesline, bunged up and loony,
older than you, cackling crazy and senile.
We bring sickbeds and credit cards,
we bring blindness and candy.

On summer nights
The south wall
Of Tim Reedy's
Tarpaper shack
Looked like a sky
Full of stars
Lamplight
Shining through
The countless
Tiny holes
He put there
Killing flies
With his silver .22

We had more than
we could use.
They embarrassed us,
our talk fuller than our
rooms. They named
nothing we could see—
dining room, study,
mantel piece, lobster
thermidor. They named
things you only
saw in movies—
the thin flicker Friday
nights that made us
feel empty in the cold
as we walked home
through our only great
abundance, snow.
This is why we said 'ain't'
and 'he don't'.
We wanted words to fit
our cold linoleum,
our oil lamps, our
outhouse. We knew
better but it was wrong
to use a language
that named ghosts,
nothing you could touch.

We left such words at school
locked in books
where they belonged.
It was the vocabulary
of our lives that was
so thin. We knew this
and grew to hate
all the words that named
the vacancy of our rooms—
looking here we said
studio couch and saw cot;
looking there we said
venetian blinds and saw only the yard;
brick meant tarpaper,
fireplace meant wood stove.
And this is why we came to love
the double negative.

Out past Sylvan Beach is the place
They still call Indian Village
Built only to be burned
The summer Spencer Tracy came to town

For years after that
Whole families would picnic there
Scavenging the debris
For rubber arrowheads

But when Spencer came
Everyone got jobs
Five dollars a day and lunch
The Depression ending with glamour

And the chance to sew on a button
For a star
Some of the men were extras
Growing beards and wearing buckskin

Rogers' Rangers looking for that passage
All summer long
From eight to five
My father was among them

And once years later
The summer after he died
I saw the movie on the late show
I stared at it hard

Even recognized a few landmarks
I scavenged every frame
For the smallest sign of him
I found none

         for Kathe

Thirsty, I turn the radio on
letting noise fill my gaps—
a country music whine,
that studs and shiplap sound,
that skeleton of feeling,
old nails pulled from boards.
Old man, father, whatever
your name, I swim
back through dust
and wood chips, back
to the summer we built
a house together and beyond,
deeper, the time you grew
a beard. I remember
the straight razor slicing
your chin. I remember
the scar you carried
to death.
            Tonight
I want everything in—
frost slowly forming
on the car roof
as if the streetlight
scattered a kind of talcum;
my homemade valentine
dangling from the light cord;

and the undertaker's breath,
pre-sweetened, his ashtray filled
with paperclips.
                    Coffee boils,
I sit back and drink
its darkness, hard times
falling with the ice.
We're taking our own
medicine again, those small
bitter pills doled out
by persimmon-faced
nurses. Hard times
music like that throb
you carried all your life,
that Depression war wound—
how the world went
cold and gray, how it
would go that way again.
You knew that icecold
freight was on the way
and knowing made you gunshy
and careful with a hammer.
There were no second chances,
a nail gone was
a nail spent.
                    I listen now
to truck stop
music getting everything
in, singing of lost
farms and the dead—

echoes, gristle music.
With your wound you
took your time that
summer. I hated
slowness and every board.
Victim of the miter box
you checked and checked,
carpenter's pencil scrawling
over every two-by-four,
testing each deceptive
number. You thought
nature lied, in cahoots
with politics. Nothing should be
easy and every calculation
must be triple-checked.
In the way and useless,
despising the dry ground,
I longed for trips
to the little store for cokes
and cupcakes and slow talk
in the cool interior
with the crazy owner.
But you kept at it
and slowly a house
rose from nothingness.
                    The music
goes on, on the edge—
like Humbird and Wiebe
in their shacks that summer,
guitars filling dusty

air with song. They played
and played and sometimes
brought over a beer
and helped lift the rafters,
half-drunk but willing.
The war was over, jobs
were hard to find
and the icecold freight
churned through those
summer fields. But
the house rose, bit by bit—
almost finished when
we moved in, tarpaper
and half a floor.
That winter we froze
and I hated it
but tried to swear
and cough like you,
tried to bang around
the kitchen mornings
before school—and played
football hard, knowing nothing
was easy.
                    In the music
I hear your saw
whine, sense your tack hammer
on the roof in little
beats. Frost is gone,
rain falls the way it did
that year when the oil heater

never gave enough heat
and I ran to the kitchen
to get dressed.
Now rain eases, ghost blossoms
unclench in strangeness.
I feel the old chill,
the hard times throb.
The neighborhood was desolate—
shacks and tents and not
a tree in sight. Like
the music Wiebe and Humbird
twanged every night
until I went to sleep.
Ancient summer uncovers
ancient summer—your
beard, your razor cut,
your scar—memory
travelling back and forth,
pacing through another rain
in hipboots and galoshes.
Buds nudge and die
in cold, the city lops trees
to stumps, and that far-off
house endures the weather
still, held up with nails
my irritation pounded
home.
        Monument enough for you—
worried into being by
your flat pencil and your

curses, a place to live,
no shrine. I learned this
and then forgot and now
it comes back: The cutting board,
the thumbed book, the worn
furniture speak our lives to us.
And I wonder if
the handmade backboard you
put up still stands.
The net shredded off
the hoop the first year
but I used it hard,
working on my left hand
hour after hour. You sighed
and swore that scarecrow
structure up as well—for me—
another monument of use
and the need to learn
Joe Fulks' jump shot.
And for a while we kept
the icy freight off
that street. It was music
and shacks and hot
summers, football and baskets.
The radio says it's lonely
time and I believe it.
The radio sobs and whimpers,
tough guys ground
to jelly. They know, they know.
With Wiebe and Humbird

I switch to wine, fed up
with unemployment checks
and coffee. Ghost trees
haunt the neighborhood. Money
for a sixpack turns up
under a flat rock. Hope
tunes our strings and pays
light bills. But we
wake to tarpaper and tents,
to empty cupboards
and jobs likely
as a royal flush.
              The icecold
freight warms up nearby
and its diesel fouls
our summer, the bad news
only war can cure.
The freight snorts and paws
like a bull, needing us.
And Truman, you said, shuffling
his deck finds some action
in Korea, and the summers
disappear. A brother of the freight
scattering dollars pulls in,
wheezing red steam. We
still live with that lukewarm
freight that mulches
everything. Humbird and
Wiebe and I listen to your
music, remembering. The old

house turns monument
and lost, and, father,

                    I

see you in your railed bed.
I trim your fingernails—
there's nothing else to do.
Your hands are thin, I.D.
bracelet so loose on your wrist.
We built a house together!
The radio sings lugubrious—
I go all the way back again,
touch that summer, that scar,
vow a beard no matter what,
dream guitars and sun,
dream hammers and studs,
dream that house from nothingness
again—our monument,
the one I hated every inch of,
the one we built together.

Now I stay awake to dream.
I invite the old times in
and they arrive clean,
free of travel grime
so honed down they're
only bone and ink,
flat dreams the needle
of the pen withdraws. That girl,
I don't even remember
her name, something like Spinks,
and the town's wild man,
Dingaling Red. They're here now
come back in pieces, free
of Cosmoline, come back from air
and the rust of thirst.
She was a neighbor's cousin
from the farm—a farm
I saw once: Cowshit
hip deep in the yard,
everything falling down.
He even called himself that,
proud of the title, Dingaling Red,
father of a friend who ate
with us and often spent the night—
a frightened little blackhaired kid
called Wart. They're all here now
insisting, faces through a fog.

She was older, maybe twelve.
She was skinny but strong
and she had a mean streak
but mainly I remember
how she rode on the pickup's
front fender, one hand on
the radiator cap, feet on the bumper.
For a while Red owned a bar
with whorehouse attached
but he went broke, gambling
and drinking his face
red as his hair. He didn't
seem to care. She rode on the fender—
it was a big family or maybe
the truck bed was full
of cowshit. Anyway that's how she rode
her ugly old man squirrelling
all over those backcountry washboards
driving like the damned fool he was
trying to make her flinch.
When they wheeled in spitting gravel
she hit the ground running
and swearing. It was a fine
thing to see. And when they left
she sat there so casually
with style and a kind of whipcord spirit
like she knew exactly what it meant.
I remember Red grinning and winking
and how his laugh seemed raw red too.
He died in a fiery wreck

and for a week the slow
drivers felt pleased with themselves
but then the beer went flat,
the war began and things
were never quite the same again.
About the girl—you know the story—
something happened and she fell off
and was killed. Everyone
said it would happen some day
and it did.

GRAVEL, ROADS, FATHERS, IDAHO, HOBOS, MEMORY

We move slowly now over gravel,
the last hint we've had of roads
in this long search for our fathers.
We hope this place is Idaho
as we were told by hobos
so far back in our memory

it's nearly lost. Or is this memory
we touch and only think it's gravel,
our path more lost than any hobo's?
Perhaps we've followed too many roads
as imaginary as the place called Idaho
where they said we would discover fathers.

But still we are without fathers
except those fading images in memory
who invented this wilderness of Idaho.
Soon enough we'll eat the gravel,
soon enough we'll abandon roads
and jungle-up forever with the hobos.

Or do we dream the hobos
as we dream our lost fathers,
night after night along these roads?
There is something in our blood, a memory
grinding like gears to produce this gravel
we scatter like seeds all over Idaho.

Give us a break, we're lost, Idaho!
We can't even find those old hobos,
and quarry as we will there's too little gravel
for the single file we need to reach our fathers!
We're drunk, confused, our memory
bulldozed and gouged by new roads.

We travel circles, not roads
and have never admitted Idaho
to the union, much less our memory.
And we carry within us strange hobos
who all insist they are our fathers
in voices harsh as gravel.

So we give up roads and gravel
and every memory of dim hobos
who lied of Idaho and our fathers.

Late at night we heard waves
suffering their slow
way from Oregon,

crawling the dust like snails,
scaling mountains, scuffling
through gulches

until we felt them in the lake
where our monster drowsed
waiting for the perfect weekend

when he would make us famous
in a Sunday supplement.
He knew the sea

and in him we knew it too.
He was an exile
from that green regime

and now he farmed our lake
masquerading as a deadhead
winking those old knotholes

in the moon-inspired waves.
Winters he spooned the arctic in—
our dogs turned white,

our dark bears
erased themselves with snow—
but the sea was always there

lapping in that inch of air,
urged across all those miles
from Coos Bay,

moving like an oyster
then surfacing again with spring,
our scoop of sea

our pool of sky
containing all the images—
the green deep,

the giant bear trap clams
of South Sea movies,
U-boat sharks

patrolling each dream,
water tigers, sea elephants
and the caped ray

cloud shadow, devil fish—
all piped into our lives
underground, by radio

and double features twice a week.
Our water glass vision
of the sea came in, a log

wearing a halloween mask,
calling our names in sleep,
pumping our blood all night.

I pack in for the night
Carrying whatever I need
In pockets and clipboard
Culling the exits for ripeness
Trying the bus marked AGE
Heading for the icehouse
I do the opposite
                              of take
Remembering the way
                                    in pieces
The path no wider
                              than a string
Every spring
                    the meadow by the icehouse
Overflowed
                  killdeer
                              moss smothering
Surfaces
                  tadpoles dotting the clear water
But the access road
                              dwindles
Down again
                  becoming this path
I scratch
                  through the deepest woods
I know
            The trees like a wall

Some green marble sweating
Bears and wildcats
Once we walked those
Marbled veins
Wandering a thickness
Suddenly lithe
Spidery with ferns
Alone I knew
The softness stiffened
And lost me like a door
Slammed shut
A closet of faces and fingers
And hot whispers
At your back
Anything could happen then
The floor go limp with snakes
And the air grip
Like muscles in a throat
With the wildcat's screech and thump
The one orange word the woods spoke
Screaming wild
                    locking the door
I drop to my hands and knees
Crawling under ferns
                              until
I touch ancient toys
Trucks and tractors
                         just blocks of rust
I find old clothes
                    a tiny
Checked jacket

I find rings
And ticket stubs
A waterlogged yearbook
Old furniture comes apart
                    in my hands
We caught tadpoles in mason jars
And now
            I walk that way again
Past the icehouse
                    and the road to school
Bob and Ruth and I
Soaked to the waist
Limp flowers
In our hands for bribes
We pass George Buck's
George who nursed
                    his sick heart
Home from town
                    twice a week
I see him walk
                then pause
Counting to sixty
He's back there as we pass
Bouquets wilting
                    pants icy
                            on our thighs
He made the finest bows
Strings so tight
                    they hummed
Now I'm sifting hard

Wilderness all around
Darkness smothering my skin
I pick up baby teeth like pennies
Lost hair like pins
So dark
        my eyes are pebbles
We shiver
          in the chill
Dreading the fever
            of kitchens
The quick heat
          of scolding air
And their father's
           tantrums
The walk is always longer than you think
It takes us by Harry Culp's
Empty house
          large and shady
So much deeper than our houses
And his toys
           were numerous with delight
But they did no good
I remember his pale skin
And the way his
          tiny arms
             jutted
From shirts
          that always seemed too big
Older
      he reached
          our size again

Then grew smaller
                    shrinking back
To babyhood to please
                    his aging parents
The last time
He was like
                    a sack of ivory kindling
In his father's arms
                    lost in the huge
Folds of striped
                    overalls
                              head lolling
Loose as a baby's
                    engineer's cap
                                   askew
I leave this neighborhood
This room
This paper
I leave the dark city
And my neighbors
                    all those sleeping
                                        irritants
I leave this and pack in
All the way
All the way
                    to the broken fields
Of fathers and sons
The dark nights of coughing
The sounds of morning
As he banged fire
                    from the iron stove

Now we hurry by the Culps'
And I drop off Bob and Ruth
And slip home
Down the hill
           hearing their father say
He'll tan their
           skinny little asses
Now I flinch
        past swamp
And hopeless mason jars
Tadpoles bleak soup
          in sunlight
Past the icehouse and the road to Boise
The exit from trees
        and freedom
Everyone said Bob's and Ruth's father
Was as cocky
        as a banty rooster
And it was true
        He stood that way
Stocky and straight
        chin high
          handy with his fists
Later
    as the war moved us west
And we forgot the town
I saw him in bed
        just milk leg
He said
Bob and Ruth looked scared

We had little to say
Later still
            we heard his mind
Went
He visited home sometimes
Playing in the yard
Like a three year-old
His children's
            youngest brother

PURSUIT

And now I follow my father
For three years
Living on crackers
Drinking from puddles
I bide my time
Watching
As he shadows the three
Who beat hell out of him
Behind Finn Hall
It is my job
I must do it right
Salty crackers biting
The sores on my tongue
Winter turning my feet
To stumps
But I hang on
As one by one
He catches them
And makes them pay

Upstairs the sanders
rubbed fingernails
thin, hands shiny
and soft as a barber's—
men past forty
down on their luck.
Below, I worked in a haze
of fine dust
sifting down—
the lives of the sanders
sifting down, delicately
riding the cluttered
beams of light.
I pounded nails
on the line.
The wood swallowed hard
nailheads like coins
too thin to pick up.
During breaks I read—
You gonna be
a lawyer, Ace?—
then forgot the alphabet
as I hammered
afternoons flat.
My father worked there too
breathing the sanding

room's haze.
We ate quiet lunches together
in the car.
In July
he quit—hands
soft, thick fingernails
feathery at the tips.

So many things happen
on trips yet all we
remember is middle—
start and finish burned
away, lost like pencil
points and erasers.
But this is okay.
Memory lights up
that old stretch of road
and I feel the rough
upholstery of my back
seat corner. They've turned
on the radio and I hear
the invaders advance on
Princeton, New Jersey—
a place much farther than
Mars—hear the speaker
conjure the pylon shadow
with panic, then
the spitting sound
of things being crushed
followed by silence,
that beautiful ominous
silence yawning all the way
to Idaho and filling
our small car with echoes.
I feel very calm

and invisible. The world
is more interesting
than I had been led
to believe. I think we'll
survive—they never mention
Idaho on the radio.
And there are no shadows,
only green hills and meadows
and the men's airless calm—
my father and his friend
saying "war" with proper
respect, my mother calm
and interested too,
but the other woman
suddenly hysterical, crying:
"My babies! My babies!"
Childhood's usual embarrassed
witness I am sad at this
and concentrate politely
on the view, pleased
with my insignificance
and sure no invasion is worth
such tears and foolishness.

Late now I follow old roads.
Gravel bites my feet.
I feel the old mystery
of culverts, the strangeness
of switchbacks and winding.
I follow one to the dump.
Another leads to the swamp
where I dredge night after night.
My dreams fill up with silt.
In sleep I travel home—
under sail, in steerage, week
after poisonous week—to waste
spaces, backroads, the unmapped
plains of hunger. My shovel
digs sod. All the travelled miles
scale down to cold wind,
the whine of aching space.
I move in darkness
nudging like a mole
through that sandy history,
all that rocky soil.
I move by rumor,
by the uneven spokes
of memory. The farmhouse
seethes with lies and money,
the hushed greed for land
rising like the smell of something

dead. It is in the tinny
water. It is in the tasteless
food. And the old man's
dying is like icy breath
across the floor the others
wade through. Outside
all the tools are scattered
and the barn unfinished—
one wall like the pattern
of a jigsaw, shiplap ends
abstractly, chewed by air,
rafters already blue and veined,
gray stacks of two-by-fours
sinking in weeds.
The old house goes cold
then lumbers slowly
to another farm
leaving only echoes
and the scar
of its single footprint.
There is no end to this
seething. Back and forth,
climbing ladders of dust,
dreaming down cold valleys,
harvesting crops of ice.
I hear the music from Finn Hall:
The sound of feet and the secret
pint smuggled in the dark,
every fight a legend.
Farther west my father

packs potatoes—all those
lidless eyes in the huge
cellar—his shoulder rubbed
raw by the kitchen bulb,
the wound a gift brought back
from his vast travels
on wings of burlap
for fifty cents a day.
Later, bears move
in the summer trees. I feel
their huge poise, leafshade
their matted fur, tub
hearts thumping patience.
No corner can be turned.
Red eyes follow every
move. At night they
amble in, dark flanks
crowd the windows black,
rank breath snorts ashes
up the flue. Helpless,
I pray for winter—
for sleep, for the snows of sleep.
We move there now,
settling, tasting familiar dust,
travellers without tickets
thrown off the train,
hobos sapped crazy
by railroad bulls.

LONELY ROADS
for Joan

What roads we followed, what interstates
of discontent, needle paths, pavements
pounded to flour to reach this room!
We trace them back tonight,
the surgical scar of that railroad
a blue line of gravel through the hills.
We follow them all finding some tangled
as string in old drawers, spread out
in our wrinkled palms, that relief
map of our lives. What dreams
brought us here? What fissures
have they crawled, what visions
of black light in the deepest fathoms
of our sleep? We trace them tonight,
each following a different route.
You go where you must—
the lonely Greyhoud, five days
of cheese sandwiches, the half a house
where your childhood lives.
I move along the Columbia,
split off toward Ontario, Weiser, climbing
away from flat heat, dinosaur hills.
And as always New Meadows sleeps
except for the single light at the depot
left on for the bugs. Climbing
I uncover old anticipations like road signs,

catch that old taste of air, thin and clear,
the old house taking shape room by room,
the town rising around me
as I climb the stairs to you
flagging down your lonely Greyhound.

BACKTRACKING

1.
The morning paper hits the porch
and all my vocabulary fades,
headlines steal every word
leaving nothing but bone.
So I play possum until evening
dreaming the ancient monster's
form dripping algae and dead
time—my words gone, the air
used up and still.
                        But when
the paper goes to bed I sweep up
syllables like a janitor until
I have them all again except
the twenty-five I leave
my disc jockeys. I even
trespass on my neighbors' words,
ready to use their bleak
utensils—their "huh's" and "I
told you so's," their grunts
and wheezes. I keep after them
all, especially the never-to-be-
spoken they ground to powder
with their teeth in sleep.

And because I can I call
the street a lake, black ice rippling,
the old algae shuffling in.

2.

Past midnight the sun rises and I
walk old ties by the mill, taking
up that stuttering gait, eating
a Jubilee candy bar. The lake's blue
bubble glistens on my left. On my
right the glinting foil of silver
storage tanks.
     Here I let the monster
rise breaking the blue glisten
of the lake,
     rise snorting and curling
like a Chinese dragon.
      All water
has its monster, that surge of rumor,
that need curdling depths
       and one summer
we found ours
    and with him
the little glory
    we could stand.

3.

The summer people never saw us
no matter where we stood. We
were audience, clammed-up witnesses,
big eyes for their boats and cars.
Somehow they owned us, allowed us
to spend our bitter winters

with their summer cabins.
                                        Before our
monster came the town was
half-asleep, dreaming through dinners,
living one day like another—
a wide place in the road.
                                        But then
we bloomed for one whole season,
the yellow glow of fame fanning
down from the lookout—
a monster made us human.

4.
All that summer we went out
in Bob's blue rowboat every chance
we got. Each deadhead grinned
like our cherished monster, the great
slimy pet we would be the first
to see. He was our own murky
creature and he dredged us up
from all our anonymous gloom
until the drugstore couldn't stock
enough copies of the Sunday supplement
that put us on the map.

5
But, no matter what I do tonight,
the lake freezes over and the summer
cabins are too far away to vandalize

or burn
        and I pull back, waiting
for the morning paper's signal,
invention running down, rubbed raw
by nights like this, the old piston
crystalized, held together with glue.

What I want is all that oblong
past—
        an old summer reeling in
drunk and disorderly,
                the summer
people and the long long legs
of their untouchable daughters,
teeth like mints, eyes like .22s,
that lake, that monster basking
and winking and nodding.
But the lake is frozen and lost—
the monster locked up for good.

Again I answer the cold phone, again
I hold my breath between each
word, again I fly
                    over snow-dusted plains.
I give up each possession. I turn off
the last light. Like a hobo I travel.
(Nameless all the lights go out.)
A bat weaves an arc like an eyelash
on the sky and all the roads
roll up. When I sleep I sleep
under bridges. When I sleep

I dream this dream.
                    Candles
in the windows die.
A scarecrow clucks his tongue.
Dead weeds beside a road draw out
a longing for the stark, the barren,
the faded lives of sticks and rocks,
husks, frozen seeds—
                    and the windows
die as well.
            No streetlight burns.
I grope my dark way back
tasting asphalt and gravel.
Road film oils my eyes.

All the lights go out.

            I follow signs—
blinkers, arrows, any hint.
Metal clinks in alleys.
Shapes flap like maimed dogs.
And again it's there
           the house
a ruin
    a shack lost in the woods,
only leaves and dust breathing softly.

Then it all twists off the page
with Thalidomide and despair.
It's been another night
of coaxing and refusal and I'm
like a mover carrying vacancy
into those rooms, a trip for each
spoon, one cup of emptiness
at a time, a single word
in each hand:
        Nothing.

Nameless
       all the lights go out,
all the roads roll up,
candles in the windows die
and the windows die as well—

house and town, the dim
ways we came
               dissolve.
It is late. We must invent
those backtrack routes—
                    without words
we lose the way—invent
every step we came, invent
words for every grand
crackpot model of our lives
built in garages and bottles.

Somehow with these words I've
got to build my own boat
in the cellar, find my visionary
chicken ranch of ease, my
beefsteak mine, my leather orchard.

I want the old swamp, the dogs
that died, sentiment smelted down
to an ore that counts
                 in the meadows
of déjà vu
          and deeper still.
A winter night
             provides the fuel.

1.
In Idaho it all ground down,
the lake seemed always
frozen. For heat
you chopped wood.
Sometimes a chip
flew in your eye. Then
you were simply a man
with one eye. Out hunting
if your best friend
shot the other one out
you were blind.
                    But toughness
was honored, some irreducible
the Depression couldn't steal.
You gave up a tooth here,
a black eye there but never
gave up the final thing.
                    To honor
this strangeness they set up
speakers at the lumberyard
and everyone drove over
for the second Louis-Schmeling
fight. Men sat on runningboards
and fenders passing a pint
around. Kids played in the sawdust

knowing enough to keep quiet
at something this important.
The whole town was there,
everyone in that ring, quivering
in the static.

We measured history
with fights: How Harvey knocked
that cheating doctor on his ass,
how the Roland boys took on
the whole town of New Meadows.
You tasted blood early, the flavor
like tears while your father
watched, his silence saying times
were tough, trouble resolved
itself hard. If you were wrong
you suffered. If you were wrong
you lost a few of vanity's rotten
teeth. If you were right you still
laid off a few days, flicking
your tongue in the gaps.

And so
we all drove over for Louis
and Conn but we don't go there
anymore. You can't let them
walk over you

but they do.

2.
Something was coming, some giant
bulldozer, some heavy equipment

nightmare bringing change.
                                   Feeling
this rumble in their nerves
some fought or drank, some
got religion, the only allegiance
available, jumping in that church
like a lake, their old thirst
making them holler, talk in tongues,
wrinkle the hell out of their Sunday
best and get down on their knees
to lick their tongues dry on that
slivery floor and wind up
begging Jesus for just one more
drink in paradise.
                         Mainly people
found hard pleasures where
they could, feeling the earth shudder,
changing partners at a dance
and never bothering with the paperwork.

But something was coming, some
March of Time voice about to announce
the end of it all for Holy Roller
and drunk. There was a hidden
frenzy
              and the giant growl of diesel
in the next valley,
                              earth movers throbbing.
It was then the hard coil within
broke up and some Elsewhere loomed

demanding allegiance,
and we felt
our legends sink away
and drift slowly
to the lake's bottom
where the sad
carcass of our monster lay,
great
cathedral ribs
empty forever.

In this winter stutter and lack
of spark, this growl of starters
in the snow grinding hard, I
give back all the words
and wonder only if the old snowcrust
in the meadow will still support
me. Can I go crosscountry
with eyelashes of frost, nostrils
freezing and thawing with each
breath? I remember the meadow,
its winter metamorphosis
but a blizzard rises here.
I go in circles, tethered to some
strange center telling me
to sleep, some spinning funnel
drawing me down. And I do
sleep, my hobo dreams fall
to crystal breaking, wine bottles
shatter on and on falling
and falling toward some pure
crystal center and in this dream
I know that we all twist
toward that vacancy, that heart
of glass, that bony crystal,
that spirit of resurrected empties,
that home of irreparable damage.
But now deep inside the dream

I find the frozen town.
A white wind creases the air,
the snow like broken glass,
and every familiar house
is vacant, roofs caved in,
walls askew, wind blasting
that vacancy. Everyone is gone!
A furious ghost town frozen
in place. I can't believe it—
to have come this far to this!—
and like an insane mailman
I seek out each one
and tick it off—*Gone, Gone,*
Gone. Winter and time have
killed each one. No blowtorch
dream can set this right.
Then I hear the crystal break
again, I hear every gritty
bit. I lose, tonight I lose
and to get back I must
invent a new alphabet
to make this world live, to keep
it from this sleep of ice.
New alphabet, new language,
new vocabulary of heat—
a language hot enough to melt
that crystal back to sand.
Hot enough to thaw
the frozen lake, hot enough
to breathe the dead back

from blast and nothingness,
hot enough to swell and build
until walls and roofs return
and all the lights go on.

Upstairs just now I stood
in the hall letting the rafters
settle on my shoulders,
listening to the sleepers,
and then fell down this page
again—
            the only snow in town.
And the mood of elegy
falls, my words soaking in it
like rags. It forms as my
neighbors do a roadblock,
the mound of grief between
Here and There.
                    The mood
of elegy falls, dusting meetings
with old friends. We talk
and smile, uncover gems
of anecdote, polish the stones
of memory from a past neat
as a display case, that
museum we visit.
                    But I feel
myself listening, always
listening for some other voice,
some other past.
                    What I hear
is like a cough at night

from an upstairs room,
some old message I never
understood, and wherever I am
I listen for such sounds—
night cries from a child
never born. I lurch toward
him, trying to capture the cause
of nightmare, the dark
comment of a cough.
                    It's for
this poem I listen, this poem
and the huge wilderness
it moves toward—the way
the woods closed darkly
behind the old house, the way
the dark breathed hard
at apartment doors.
                    I stand
in the hall again and feel
the yokes of the rafters settle.
I keep the house together
through this deep winter,
but for pay I want a long ride
by Greyhound and then travois.
The long hard ride
until I reach that other
winter and high country,
until I pass the timberline
where the world becomes
rock and ice—a place

higher than any we have known,
higher than rafters and pages,
higher than every destination.

My buddies breathe dust
Where the rubber plants die
The lobby of the Lotus Hotel
Rooms $5 and up
                    You can see them there
Any time
            our mirror shadows

But tonight is special
                    This is their club

The hub that draws them on rainy
Nights like this
                    The murky light suits them
The dry ferns
                    The streaked glass suit them

First of course is the social hour
And for those without muscatel or tokay
There's a coke machine that works
Sometimes
Later
        chili dogs and beer for the faithful
A talcum of dust rises
From the hairless sofa
                        and every chair

Sinks low as a bucket seat

"Drive to your heart's content
There ain't no speed limit here"

The chairman says
                    beaming
Everyone likes him
They voted for his thin hair
And the little broken veins
Around his nose
                    A man like that
Is honest

They gab and sulk
                    each member
Bringing out his past
                    like a snapshot
"I could've made a go
But the location was lousy"
"That woman took every fuckin cent I had"
"He cheated me blind"
"Sonofabitch"

They like this but as the wine goes round
They grow feisty
                    grinning and nodding
As they talk of heroes
                    Ex-pugs rocking
On their heels
                    The runner-up
The hot rookie who
                    the chairman says

"Succumbed to the sophomore jinx
They curved him to death"
Someone yells "Winners never quit
And quitters never win"
Everyone roars
                    "Shee-it" the chairman whoops
Dancing a jig and hooting
And now they know everyone is there
They love the list
                    sweeter than any menu
Contenders with glass jaws
                            patsies
Masters of the bonehead play
Wrong-way Roy
                    Bums-a-month
Sluggers buried in the minors
Men over the hill
                    and out of gas
Pitchers who lost it
                    All the tragic flaws
Doctor Strangeglove
The strike-out king
                    oh yes especially
The strike-out king
This is the losers' caucus
"But come on down" they yell
"We ain't particular
There's plenty a room for you"

The old one, ungainly, out of place
        sits by the back door, sides
streaked with old meals, buttons
        carrying old fingerprints
away—tomorrow to Union Gospel.

It was my mother's stove, our
        companion for fourteen years,
collaborator on how many meals?
        Burners black and still, oven
going cold in the weather, dead clock

deader still. Once it was her
        new stove, hers for a year
before her death at forty-five—
        clearly not good enough to keep
her alive, but good enough to

carry me this far, to forty-six
        in this kitchen where I sit
dreaming back and forth, consulting
        that dead clock and those
dark burners with no news of food—

only memories going back to a day
        in winter when the stove, unnoticed,
became ours. I remember the last
        drive to the hospital, my father
driving, my arm over the seat

to hold her hand, holding as if pulling
      her along, holding as if keeping her
from falling some great distance—
      towing her dry hand all the way.
I remember how my arm went

numb, how I wanted it to sleep
      and hurt, to somehow pay and buy
her back with stupid pain. There was
      her dry hand and her eyes
and that drive going on and on

yet too short. And there was that truck
      of junk leading us—old refrigerators,
old stoves, battered and rusty—which
      I tried to stare away but it
continued, bearing its trite symbols

of the obsolete, our culture's silly
      signs of death, and all the while
her new stove waited at home,
      shiny, guaranteed for years
and years to come...

The dream searches its own pockets seeking
what feeds it well, struggling or flowing
it moves across mountains, navigates
dry riverbeds, moving with its own will
wordlessly toward its nourishment—
skunk cabbage and the swamp behind
the old house, winter melted to tea.
                                    It wants
origin and seed and plows toward
its old constituency, its gods of rubber
and tin, assuming like water its own
level.
            And as it moves words follow
in wagons, in caravans. They follow
the dream's footprint blaze, uncovering
the old right of way, that smothered trail
where words must go.
                          The dream dances
and juggles. Darts like a radio signal.
Conjures dead life from nothingness and grit.
Dream finds its ways and means,
winding up all its loose ends, tracing
arteries and veins in the body electric.

But tonight and any night the riverbed
is all words have and they travel
that trough east, willing water into it,

began—the swamp behind the old lost
house.
        I work that liquid with my hands
feeling its ropes of current, its motion
like earth-shift, like birth saying Yes,
saying No.
           But now the dream slips the hook,
abstractions take no bait and disappear
in the Oregon night of steelhead dreams,
ghost salmon, soluble trout
                    in the invented river
of words.
         And again I balance my dear sleepers
like a juggler, thinking their rooms to
the second floor by levitation, by will
and ink.
         Foraging the enamel night I wander
to the window, reread a friend's letter, check
a date—all fillers, all acts for the end
of the page—and the night gapes frosty
and clear, ice feeding on the roofs of cars,
the neighborhood seeming to thicken as it draws
closer in the cold, smothering my province,
my vacant house before dawn.
                  Somewhere the old
lake trembles, a brilliant sun-glitter on its
waves
        and far-off, its leash broken, the dream
skirts the old fringe of town, nosing and searching,
stopped short by each familiar—each rock

and tree a close friend. One and one and one,
burgeoning toward avalanche, swelling with the ancient
dead, burgeoning, every impulse sprouting, each
signature of each thing booming and rattling
like gravel from a truck peppering down, everything
finally coming in with a crazy shotgun blast
and the dream at last cries its ecstatic uncle!

1.

I need a new car every night
and each one must be
vintage '33 or 4, scavenged from
Alaska Junk just before
the giant crusher makes them
bite size.

           I sneak in and make those
old buggies talk, sorting nuts
and bolts, scouring the city
for parts.

           The extravagance of my
poverty knows no bounds.

2.

The best night I found nearly
all the parts of the '34 we
drove to Coos Bay after Pearl
Harbor. I dredged it out
and got all the way to ice
and Idaho, past New Meadows
and nearly to the farm
before its tinfoil body crumpled.
Good American something in me
died when my resurrected roadster

quit. I felt that inner crumbling,
radiator hose
          and aorta
the same flesh.

3.
But I find others,
          hotwiring Hudsons
up on blocks for twenty years
and they work.
          On blocks they
gallop and canter
          going faster
and faster
          until they hit the good
lost road.
Studebaker Reo Model B—
all gathered in the darkness,
all waiting for some greasy-
fingered judgment day.

4.
And so hunting nuts and bolts,
scavenging the body shops, plucking
the rust-ridden from the crusher,
I find suitable transportation—
the kind I like. And most

of them use cartridge ink, ink
fuels the headlights too, headlights
drawing the map I follow.
And they can change at will,
becoming boats or kites, even
submarines. It makes no difference.
The avenue is words—we're
conveyed by the streetcar of words,
the sea-going tram of syntax.

5.
Now I travel the crease in
the map,
the folds much more
convincing than those squiggle
roads.
          I pour down a fold
arriving where it meets another
fold,
then veer off toward
the center—
                    that secret interior
of maps
              where all travellers
converge.

6.
But the place is like a grease
trap and I head back
to Alaska Junk seeking

the instructions of rust,
the bland hints of dissolution.
I wander foothills of junk,
their icy shadows falling.
Something must turn up
and then, yes, I spot my ace—
the old Galloping Goose linked
with the local interurban
way down at the bottom
of the deck. Even from under
those tons I snake it out easily.

7.
Soon we're travelling hard,
grinding through wheatfields,
skidding and bouncing across
mountains, making our own
secret tracks, bell clanging
like hell. We barrel the whole
way full throttle, the Goose
finding rails anywhere it
looks, its little wheels sculpting
them from sand and rock,
the bell going crazy the whole
way announcing
                    We're Here!
We're here!

NICKEL AND DIMED
for Joan

Tonight we have the steady meter of the furnace
and the cold clear night rising forever
above the house. We have the dog lying in his pool
of quiet, we have our books and breathing—
the filaments breathing back and forth between us
as we read the evening up, read on and on
forever in these moments. Our street is stock-still
and the universe held between thumb and finger
like a nickel.
                    But we're travellers even now
as the house churns our landscape flat as a coin.
Indian heads and buffalo dot our plains, all the coins
that bought this evening so long ago:
                              Tips for errands,
dimes for movies, even the grand clanking silver
for hamburgers and shakes, all the coins that have
passed through our fingers without a trace.
                                   Moving now,
while we sit stock-still, the house seems to mint
them all again, the night a clatter of loose change
and every coin covers a date, spending the past away.
Every coin icy and ready to hold our eyelids down,
every coin says I'm part of a jackpot family, every
coin puts our trust in god but settles for cold cash
and a receipt.

The house moves through this sea.
Memories are spent money and our past is scattered
everywhere in a million tills and pockets, lost in the slots
of machines, flipped down bottomless wishing wells—
but now we travel over all these reminted coins, the house
going so fast we're standing still until we sleep.

In dreams we move on wheels, our old crackpot roadster
printing money as it goes, cat's paw tires making
counterfeits too true to be believed and our journey
back is over this landscape of money—all the coins
gone out of circulation, silver dollar and Buffalo nickel,
Indian head penny. Our tires punch them out like cookies.
The landscape of money blooms, coins turning red and blue
like poker chips that stack themselves in crazy mesas.
It is that dream
                          of the nasal sound of cash the summer
people brought when they bought the lake in June,
the dream we never talked about though it burned all
winter like a low fever, the dream of Chris Craft
and Evinrude. Those boats cut furrows in the lake
but their owners never saw below their wakes nor could
they know what we knew was there—doom and ecstasy,
ghosts of friends, our wide-eyed monster; nor could
they ever know how winter snapped all that tremble
shut with ice and how the lake stayed that way
until the winning bet broke it up in spring;
nor how we hated as we smiled their fever money
across our counters all summer.

222   Now those summer people sleep around us, wearing
their winter skins, making reservations for sand and water
in their dreams, polishing their boats edible, gritting
their teeth in sleep to keep their cabins whole
until July. We're all like bears sleeping through our
winter hours and sighing as our skin goes pale, losing
its dark memory of August, strangers to everything beyond
our double locks. With dog ears we hear the hibernating
whimpers, the nightmare wars all along the street
and we long too for the old lake, the place not called
home that is home, the place our wooden nickels take us,
the place so spent it's disappeared.

Some nights you travel back taking the whole
house, snail that you are, house-proud as you are,
calling it the big backpack, and you rumble over
money landscapes, scattering that gravel of nickels and
          dimes
wildly, the souped-up house spitting gravel.
But other nights, alone, you must crawl from one parking
meter to another buying back the past a half an hour
at a time, nickel and dimed to the poverty of nothingness.

We want the hard light of the dark,
the light struck from nothingness
and need, the light where no light is,
the impossible light of dead bulbs.
And so we move beyond water,
beyond trees, the great owl of the dark
toward some grainy piece of what
was lost, that diamond of gristle.

Tonight the trip is farther back.
I dig loam and find rusty
cans and The Sweet Singer of Michigan.
But the drive is deeper than irony.
I dig my loam and yours as foxfire
stumps dream forges, mills burgeon
in grave mounds and we reach
a clearing in the woods, some hobo

jungle—
        I meet my father there
and our hands freeze together
on boxcar rungs through the Blue
Mountains. Of course we want the lost,
the lost so near, surrounding us
like an extra atmosphere, like that icy
air we breathed in the mountains,

our knuckles frozen to those rungs
waiting for summer.
                        Now I pick my way
walking high grass, then forest,
then the swamp
                        with its usual treachery.
The dark bleaches slowly
                        to summer light,

the rungs release my hands
and everything is almost there.
I breathe softly until
                        it grows its
third dimension
                        turning from paper
to its old solidity,
the summer we

dreamed
            fastened to that boxcar.
But here it must be nursed
with caution
                        a kind of foreplay
within a dream.
                        Everything is still
the shadow-work of memory pumping
itself to roundness. Meadow
and swamp emerge. The sun plants
itself and invents the rest.
                        Meaning

sparks like downed wires—
                        some ropey force
spun from fibers too fine to braid,

some link giving a form that crumbles
as I touch its edge.
                        All this midnight
travel, this journey from winter,
leads to the shapeless shape, the salad
of meanings, this pick-up-sticks voyage
arrives at this wide place in the road,
this woods, this lake

                        and a summer day
we saw frog and snake
                        joined
at the snake's mouth.
Our knuckles thaw
                        and we climb down
from that boxcar. For such

journeys every map is completely
white—with ice or vacancy—
and folded in that intricate way
but without a single mark.
We must invent terrain and route,
ink our fuel, chair and table
our pioneer utensils,
                        our Conestoga biplane.

With them I meet the swampy
summer, melt winter from my
fingers, see snake and frog transformed
ready for their place on my flag.

I go back to the round table,
spinning its perimeter, swimming
its familiar grain and feel
the end is coming on, destination
preparing itself like a dinner,
like a kink in the road.
But zero falls and falls, the past
torn to this confetti, this frozen
dust of bones falling. With the snow
a maze descends, the map again
its old labyrinth invention,
syntax turned rubbery and loose,
aging, sentence and phrase
arthritic with remorse and ice,
our used-up language fallen to coma.
But enough of diagnosis!
Wake up the language! Without
words we lose the way for good.
Warm it ready by the old
heater. Let it get up with Slim
and bang in the black stove
with kindling. Let it boil thick
and bitter as the coffee he
thawed his bones with and turned
his brittle hands soft enough
to break six eggs in that inch
of bacon grease. We need words

228

at least as tough as those
rubber eggs freckled with pepper.
And so in the heart of winter
I thaw the words this way,
thaw until winter edges toward
spring and ice escapes my
marrow-ink and it flows
finding its way to the door
and out for a night of travel
toward those ancient summers
and the powdery earth of July,
the talcum of dust, all the ground
bones of the royal animals.
And once again the earth is dusty
by the mill, earth ground to this
nothingness by the crusher
at Cascade Road & Gravel.
Now I see the dirt by the depot
where the ground cleared first
in spring. I finger the dust
and speak at last for everything lost.

RUINED CITIES

Here are some things
you should know: First
if you come here
be ready to spend long
days in thought, long days
indoors, deeper indoors
than you've ever been.
In the steady sweet
rain you'll get beyond
the anterooms of thought,
you'll explore rooms
you've never seen.
You should know as well
that all this rich green
always loses to the gray.
Even the winter roses
fade, even the camellias
fail—or seem to under
that sky. It's the low
sky that's always there,
that knitted cap. If
you want to stay
learn to wear it
from October on. Wear
it as you explore
those neglected rooms
you boarded up so long

ago. Learn to delve
and consider, learn to test
each thing you think
you love. And even
on clear days you must
know that the mountains
you can almost touch
don't care—mainly they
display their vast
indifference just as,
to the west, the Pacific
remains aloof, clearly
representing a system
of values beyond your
pettiness. But come, walk
the trails, go out among
that green, follow rivers—
but be ready to think
of all those things you
shelved for years. Force
those doors and find
those caustic packages—
unwrap them here,
poke and shudder at
what you see, believe
it finally and learn
to live the life you have.

We sit sheltered in the dim
light and work this light
for what it's worth,
work around the jukebox, the murmur
at the bar. We sift
the noise to find our level
and the words we need.
Some burn in the candle.
Some crack with the cue ball
in the back room. We fumble
with the rest among peanuts
on the table, sifting husk and meat,
searching this weak light,
the world flaking down with the rain
outside, with the TV news, with the surly
bartender, the pool balls
knocking their heads together over
and over. We sift it all to find
our voices, the ones we used to have,
and with the second pitcher
they show up—clear, discernible,
knifing corridors through the smoky noise,
making sense in that old way
we thought was lost.
We float and drift a while, somehow
back home though we scarcely
move, somehow back *there*

with the furniture of nostalgia
and the people we once were,
thinner, braver, counting pennies
for one more glass. And this is why
we come here now, why we lose
to bar dice, to liar's poker
and the slaughterhouse cries of songs.
We have companions here—the people
we used to be. We drink with them
until we reach this level buzz
of sentiment and our tongues
grow athletic with mystery and wit
outside of time. It's then we say
what the hell and order
another pitcher, the night already
too good to waste on sleep.

You search all summer, wearing holes
along the creases of your maps,
making camp here and here, dreaming,
hoping through the chill nights.
But morning reveals the littered park,
the postcard views, the dripping tap.
So you move on, speedometer keeping track,
engine more obedient than any dog
as you look and look with shaded eyes
across countless vistas beside roadside markers,
countless parks and beaches too numerous
to remember. And you always come home
disappointed, the car's paint faded, your nose peeling,
the exhaustion of play weighing your limbs.
It wasn't there. It wasn't there again.
And you settle down to dream
the routine of home, and it's then
in dreams, or better, just before you sleep
that it rises clear, like a name carried
on the tip of your tongue all day.
Then you follow the right path
through the woods, past the burned-out shack,
the smell of skunk and death. You follow
as your limbs float out to sleep, follow past
the dump, the smoldering tires, and come finally
to the house of tarpaper, the house

of lethargy and curses where the chickens lived
indoors and the dog was called
Nuisance, where your friends, the kids, stared
fiercely out and dared you to live your life.

SOME HOUSES
for Matthew, David, Kirsten

Tonight I wander those vacancies,
hear the hollow sounds,
the protests of ghost hinges, try
to pry up windows
painted shut, scratch dirty glass
to see ourselves within, living
hard and clear in the flower
of the past. Most you never knew
and even for me their
outlines pulse in and out
of vision, roofs in dotted lines
pale as plans drawn with a nail.
Some are gone for good, true
ghosts above a parking lot,
some have moved and I can't
find them anywhere. Each held
our lives though, cupped fast
against nightmare and weather,
each swirl and eddy of our days
swirled and eddied there.
Too many now to list—
but take this one, one of the ghosts:
Driving by I still see it
etched on the air, its simple lines
still there. Every mirror was

ready with our faces, the beds
molded to the postures
of our dreams. Or this one,
surrounded by trees.
I see it packed with our days,
each act compressed, each word
compacted and stored. Even our dreams
swirl there in tight spirals.
Each place is such a warehouse,
our years labeled like a file
with its address, pain and love,
the afternoons and nights
we swam through turned solid
and our lives imprinted there the way
ancient ferns, traceries of shells
and flowers, are drawn on stones.

In time they fade away into
a kind of suburban haze
on the outskirts of your life—
you know they're there
you just never see them now.
The result, though, is that they
always seem to be children
and you're sure those cards
you sometimes get showing them
with children of their own
are clever fabrications. Actually
they're just dressing up again
in their parents' clothes, playing
house the way they did at seven.
In fact the more you think
about them the younger they get
while you unfairly keep
getting older by the minute—
as you study those age spots
on your hands they seem
all freckles and pigtails.
Clearly it is unfair how
your memory peels their years
away and pulls your aging body
back to all that vague intensity
you felt on visits—so close,
so intimate, yet strangers too

with lives that went on nicely
without you when the visit
ended. If you called one now
you know a child would answer.

The last time I saw him
he was still playing drums
in the dance band at Stover's,
the family ne'er do well still
going strong at seventy-five.
Everyone else was dead—
all his hard working brothers,
all those who said he would
never amount to a hill
of beans. But there he was,
a round smiling man,
keeping the beat on the bass,
sticks flirting across the snare,
traps and cymbals working
four or five hours a night
in that rich dance hall
gloom, doing what he liked
as he always did.
                                His house
was a dusty museum
of fiddles and banjos, every
instrument but a piano,
and poles, tackle, guns.
The clutter was marvellous—
all that glittering intricacy,
whorled saxophones, the wasp
waists of fiddles, immaculate

rifles with stocks so oiled
and burnished and dark
they looked like pools you
could sink your hands into,
box after box of spinners
and lures, subtle little flies
clinging to hooks. In spite
of bachelor's dirt each of these
things shone.
                    I never much
liked him—he was arrogant
even toward children, a boastful
cocky little man who
loved to tease until he
drew tears—but I like him
now and see a little into
those polished stocks, see how
he chose his life and built
it up around himself,
a life of sparkling horns
and delicate fiddles, a life
of rods and reels and guns
carefully gathered to give
his days a shape he liked.
He outlived all the lovers
of the grindstone doing as he
damn well pleased, playing
hard until he was eighty
and saying goodbye on the bandstand,
a fishing trip planned for the morning.

LELA AND OTHERS
for Kirsten

Tonight you are away sleeping
in sea breeze, dreaming I think
of horses, and I remember
the other day when we
went through the old album,
remember talking as best I could
about that random evidence,
all circumstantial or less.
I knew most of the faces
but the occasions were lost—
Aunt Jenny shading her eyes
and standing on a rock
in the lake. Her dark ship
finally came in, I know, but why
was she there with black hair
and a trim figure I can't
recall?
       We smiled at the pictures
of my father that my mother
cut in half, scissors trimming
away an old girl friend.
Was it Lela? The mysterious Lela,
the album's Madame X,
who turned up so often
in the early pages and then
dropped from sight for good?

There is always a Lela—
but who is Lela?—looking
as helplessly young as my father
looked at twenty-five.
       More
evident even than Lela
was that cousin I never liked
who squinted at us from page
after page as if the album
were a chronicle of his
life in the sun. He's gone too—
a bad death in California.
       We looked
at all the relatives on all
those lost days standing
by their cars as if pretending
to leave or arrive, car doors open,
feet poised on running boards.
In the pictures of the farm
there was an odd formality—
no clowning, no bottles tipped
to mouths, no uncles' hats
on children—the men
looking away from the camera
with their large bare arms folded,
aloof and distant.
       There was that one
we both liked: Your great grandfather
in a sepia field beside plow horses
and your grandfather in the middle

distance, the whole somehow
telling us of the brown mystery
of the lost, those powerful docile
Dobbins, those strong men gone
to dust.
       Then a turned page caught
my breath—your grandmother
scarcely older than you are now.
I remembered every feature
and how they grew hazy
those last days.
       We went through them
all and I became garrulous with
the garrulous uncle, tough and wild
with that crazy cousin, cunning
with one aunt, tight-fisted with another,
and spoke sotto voce of that great aunt
who went bad in Butte, Montana—
the whispered family skeleton, no longer
even a whisper.
       I felt them all converge
with their broken stories and the past
with Lela's slim hand gripped
my wrist an instant then let go.
And our past mingled in, offering up
my memory of your birth
and how some long tension, some
crimped deep fiber in me
relaxed for good when you arrived.

ROGERS' RANGERS,
A LATE REPORT

Like my father I'm
an extra, like
him I disappear
from the final

cut, edited out,
coiled on the cutting
room floor,
my one walk-on

dark and swept
away with his
janitor's broom.
But we're together

at least, relaxing,
smoking and talking
in the warm
gloom of the boiler

room among shadows
and dust, among
spiders and push-
brooms, the rags

of our profession.
Soon enough we'll
empty ourselves
with the trash

and whoop home
with a six-pack
glad to be anonymous
and transient,

glad to have a room
and time and names
that are ours alone
and an address

forever unknown.

You know what kinds of hats
we wear but do you know

we haul in extra rocks
for our fields? Can you imagine

how much we hate your
soft hearts, your paperbacks,

your two-minute eggs? If you
dare to come here beware of the hard

labor of our mercy. But we
can get along without you.

One of us makes a nice living
by drilling holes in roofs,

another plows ruts in the road.
Two brothers do very well with

found sculpture—they put
old engine blocks and rusty

car bodies in our yards.
Do you know what we call

our town? Between a Rock
and a Hard Place of course.

We feel nothing but contempt
for all that's bituminous.

A LITTLE NIGHT MUSIC

With relief I hear my neighbors fight—
one sign of life

on a dark night.
Listen, they slam every door they have,

whine and scream,
throw dishes.

I love the way
they dig deep in their throats

for new voices,
growl and caterwaul,

digging under words to find
their passion's true sound.

Now we have a secret bond.
We belong to the same hard club,

true users of the night
filling lank hours

with the hoarse music
of love.

Daily we have the sea's commentary,
that large green voice
rising and falling, speaking her
lonely Greek hour after hour.
At sunset she takes the sun quickly
and we walk the sand
in darkness listening to that gloss
on our days, that muttered
interpretation we thought we
understood—salt and water, pressure
and release. We listen sifting
for those cries and drums, the voices
of something lost, our own
voices out there. We listen these days
away as our past sifts through
our fingers—all the times
we've walked this sand and heard
the surf knock its wind out
beating hard on the shore, and watched
lights come on in the houses,
the sea lion lift his head
like a dog and carry on
his silent dialog. But tonight
we feel a change, some shifting
of sands and birds we can't
explain, a wind swerving

out of the east, a darkness deeper
than we remember. The sea lion
is gone, the surf continues
its gibberish, and we are alone here
in a way we never knew before—
each of us walking apart, parsed,
with fog coming in, the moon lost,
direction scattered everywhere, the sea
pounding her fists on the sand and weeping.

Some are like those obscure receipts
kept in your wallet for years,
now illegible, the paper so thin
it tears at each fold

and you can't remember
what the paper meant or why you've
saved it so long and for what purpose.
But those deaths are with you,

intricately folded and flaking,
and you feel that way too,
pocketed, useless, aging
and saved for no purpose.

But there are others, the legends:
Your grandfather walking
through that blizzard along the rope
hooked to the barn

finding his final pneumonia
at the end. And your invisible uncle,
Baby Danny, whose death
your grandmother carried

like a purse full of rocks
all her life
until it became the knapsack that
rounded her shoulders down

to her final silence.
And here we come to all those
pictures—young men with mustaches
and derbies, girls with waists too thin

to be believed, hair swept up
like sea waves and skin
truly like cream, and the children
cheeky and freckled—

all dead. Dead the spotted terrier
sitting up, the patient plowhorse,
the cat called Lucky.
And you carry them all—

your crumpled and folded
legends, your bag of rocks,
your cracked brown receipts
for bills, paid and unpaid.

There are many tonight and the rink
is like a Breughel, such motion
and animation, at first glance
some busy microcosm.

Above the rink I lean on the rail,
my sleeve settling in the residue
of a sticky drink and on the rail
beside it, scatched: *Letitia*

loves Spud. Below, the skaters
circle crazily, looking now like
a swarm but soon you begin
to see that two types stand out:

The helpless scarecrows so tenuous
and bad they command the attention
they fear—you can almost
hear them pray for balance.

The others you notice of course
circle with such skill they seem
to fly. They skate with their hands
behind their backs and show

enormous deference by giving the inept
berths wide enough for ships.
In truth they're in their element,
a kind of royalty down there

but so good that they're benign.
Like royalty they know they need
the awkward to set them off.
One cuts an elaborate figure

of concern for a fallen child
showing he's not only good on skates
but good at heart. Another averts
what we're meant to believe

is a disaster with arms thrown up
and a nifty shift when a scarecrow
falls twenty feet away.
                        Thinking
of Letitia and Spud who were moved

to pledge their love right here, I realize
the Breughel swirl below just may be
a little version of the world though
all the gestures seem too large,

like a silent movie—mimed
danger and concern, pratfalls,
the rubber-kneed drunks, bad
music in the background,

and love pledged in the balcony.

In the heart"s fist we knew
nothing lived, the world
with its promises roamed away—
every tree wanted to die,
every blade of grass longed
for winter, and love of course
was all a dusty snare.
So we hit the brakes on that
icy stretch by the river
and roared as the car began
its graceful crazy turns
worried only about spilling our
cradled quarts. Remember
how the trees swept by and we
somehow missed the ditch
every time around? Five
was the best we did, three
was average.
                At parties
we foraged for arguments,
near rage at some new-found
dirty trick of fate,
and shouted down anyone

who said he wanted to fly
but had no head for heights.
Then we stormed away
looking for night"s deepest
corner, its sharpest curve,
hitting ninety-five on the road
from Estacada, throwing
empties at the sign posts,
or hit the brakes again
and laughed as the car began
its lazy circles, always
hoping for six.
                    We longed to hit
something—face, abutment, god—
and dared every ditch and pole
to meet us half way, c3ertain
we were made of coiled steel
and would live in this dusty
world forever, but we wound up
so fast! We needed all this, you see,
not for you but for us. We needed
a wilderness but had found none. Which is why
that room where hope and beauty
join hands, that room where each
expectation is realized. And it knows
no limits, growing larger as you

walk in, its parquet spreading
out and out beyond the Roman bath
and solarium, beyond tennis court
and garden. It has no bounds.
See the baseball diamond. The golf course.
And somehow it was always there,
somehow we never got around to opening
that door though we passed it every
day for years, and it was always there
opening forever on the limitless
extravagance of the world.

We invented these trees and mountains, that long gash
of gulley tumbling toward the lake.
By main force we brought each rock into being,
each of a different size and shape, each carved
into its dim life by us. We squinted that mica
from nothingness through our eyelashes and pulled
each giant fir from the ground with tweezers—
each begining thinner than a hair but we
nursed them up with curiosity and the weak strength
of our thin fingers. Before we came
none of this was here—all the ferns and brush
were made with pinking shears. We shoveled
every lake and compelled water
to bear the fruit of fish. With our pens we drew
the creeks and nudged bear and deer from deep shadows.
None of this was here before we came.
We invented these trees and mountains,
conjured each pebble and boulder, shaped
those rough peaks with our hands, nursed those
great trees up and up from the near nothingness
of hairs. A whiskbroom and moonlight
made cougar and wildcat, dry sticks and dust
the snake and mole, with rain and mud we made
beaver, wood chips formed eagle and hawk we whittled
so fast! We needed all this, you see,
not for you but for us. We needed
a wilderness but had found none. Which is why

we invented this lovely one just here
between Thompson and Brazee in Northeast Portland.
Our love, you see, demanded such a setting.

In your dream, desperate, with guests
at the threshold, suddenly
you remember the other room, pristine
and perfect, the one
we've never used. And just as
suddenly there is the door
we've overlooked for fourteen years,
somehow missing it day
after day, and you open it
and there is the other room
glorious and clean, the sheets crisp
as new money, the furniture without
blemish, and the paint fresh
as paint. This is the guest room
to end them all, a room almost
too good for guests, a veritable
museum of a room, defining
in fact what a room
should be. And the wonder!
It's been there all along as we scuffled
and cleaned, as you painted
and scraped, as we sweated
to clear a place for our unknown guests.
But here it is, that ideal room,
that room posing for pictures, that dream
room that goes a hundred miles
an hour on no gas at all,

that room where hope and beauty
join hands, that room where each
expectation is realized. And it knows
no limits, growing larger as you
walk in, its parquet spreading
out and out beyond the Roman bath
and solarium, beyond tennis court
and garden. It has no bounds.
See the baseball diamond. The golf course.
And somehow it was always there,
somehow we never got around to opening
that door though we passed it every
day for years, and it was always there
opening forever on the limitless
extravagance of the world.

This morning there was another one
Looking used but not worn out
Beside the road
What do they mean?
Do people just abandon them at sixty
On the freeway
Suddenly tired of a single shoe?
Are they some secret sign?
Are they just the shoes
Of careless drivers
Dangling one foot out the window?
Do they belong to insomniac passengers
Who can only sleep
With their feet in the open air
One shoe falling off in a dream?
What do they mean?
What are they trying to say?
And this afternoon that pair
(Pairs are unnatural)
Of high heels thirty feet apart
But one was red the other brown.
Imagine what you want—
Are they all that's left of walkers
Single vacant tokens?
Are they obscure milestones?
Hex signs?

But how are they lost?
What carelessness prevails
Allows single shoes to fall from sealed cars?
Do they contain desperate messages
Like bottles?
Was each filled with wine and passion
And thrown away
To seal deep intimacies?
Are they placed there
By itinerant princes
Looking for the right fit?
What do they mean?
They come in all sizes
Their tongues loll
They look helpless
What do they mean?
So desolate so empty
So hungry without their feet.

I sat silent in the back row too
Feeling sleep and the room's buzz
Settle their nets
Even now I drift there
Over the scrape of chairs
Shedding lectern and notes
Travelling back
To an old self
Sleepy with rage in the last row
Save me a place
As far back as possible
Where faces haze anonymous
A place beyond questions
Where all answers curdle
And turn inside out
Where we stay alive by mockery
And the need only to be present
But scarcely counted scarcely known
Save me a place
I sit there too
As nearly erased as possible
Sleeping with both eyes open
Champion of the doodle
Master of the concealed yawn
Silent assassin
Save me a place

Beyond charm and winks
Too far away
To polish anyone's apple
I understand how to snort
Contempt with silence
How to be and not be
How time is a stone
That never moves

AT FOUR IN THE MORNING

Outside just now the birds began
their tentative hymns
to the sun, nearly sure
it will come up again. But what I want

on this June night is the hymn
to you—the one so long strangled, so long
caught in my throat, the tongue-
tied one. Such things

should be simple, I know—
like stream water over stones,
like breeze in summer leaves.
But even there the contrary

shows—stone and water, wind and tree.
And I want it not to be simple—
I want storm and calm,
I want the true voice of sentiment

and rage, of rising and falling,
the spirals of love, curve, dead spot,
the soaring, the earth-bound.
Yet how is this possible? Only this way.

Every line, wherever it went,
has been yours. Other things

are nobody's business. All the lines—
as tonight when we waited

for the sealant to cure
the radiator's disease and looked
in the rug store window. As tonight when
we talked over beer. As tonight

when we watched the new TV.
As tonight when we spoke of our children.
As tonight when we rummaged the dark
closets of ourselves again for love.

> *Pray, how is it that you have grown so thin?*
> *Is it because you suffer from poetry?*
>   —*Li Po to Tu Fu*

I spend the night shuffling
old lines, those yellowed sheets,
all that calligraphy
of error. So many journeys
begun in the dark, so many
lost quests. But sometimes
it works, sometimes the words
rise like fish volunteering
for the hook, fish so deep
you didn't know they
lived—as Lu said. Yet tonight
the journey is dim,
the lighting indirect, and I
know again Lu's description
of the six senses stranded
and the heart lost
when the poet is motionless
as a petrified log, dry
as a desert river. Is it
any wonder Li Po drank?
Gulches are dry places
to travel and the poet is
always sure every river
wants only to run dry, all that
coolness turned to dust

and alkali. And so poets
drink or otherwise kill
time that's out to make them
flop helpless in their own
dust. At heart they're accountants
and scholars of sound,
but they flop around and get
in trouble by insulting
the right people, rolling their
eyes like pinball machines.
That isn't the poet though—
that's the beached fish
between poems flailing against
the melodrama of the empty
page, trying to embarrass
the muse into coming across
just one more time
in the midst of this same
old rudderless nada.
Lu Chi knew and said flatly:
Eloquence is hard to find.
But he knew, too, that
however it limped
writing was Being drawn
from the Great Void, sound
rung from Profound Silence, and that
a sheet of paper, even this
lined notebook page,
carries the Infinite

just as a panorama is somehow
squeezed from the inch-space
of the heart. When this happens
the poet swims and dives
with giant lungs. The dry river
flows deep and fish leap
for his hooks. Every flying
dream comes true, every
ugliness is beautifully
ugly, every dreary hour is alive
with the truth of dreariness,
longing and homesickness
come home. Inevitably
the line goes slack of course, that
kite pull gone, the river
dwindles back to dust
and brings the first tickle
of thirst, the first hint
that the private dust bowl
muse is back in town.
And now, Lu, I look
for my "rallying whip"
to snap these words in place
and make them serve,
shaking off this dust.
It's time for the river's
transfusion, time for
midnight's resurrection
when, as you said, the poem

pounds virtue on brass
and nourishes like mist.
Without song we lose the way,
without song we fall
through the Great Void toward
Profound Silence. Without words
there is only darkness
and the dry rivers
of our streets. Lu, I try
now to swim through this
dust, looking for the still
moment when I may name
the misty rain that nourishes
these dusty streets awake.

Everyone knows there are those
Who eat best from empty plates

Glasses of air
Sustain them well

They love the elegance
Of bare cupboards

Such cupboards have the austere
Look of Danish modern

Mother Hubbard
Is their patron saint in fact

And their tables are always cleverly set
With the condiments of absence

Where savor has lost its salt
Everyone knows that life is truly spritual

Everyone knows there are those
Who are warmed by cold stoves

After all imagined fire
Is always hotter than real fire

Such paradoxes are
Their true life blood of course

Everyone knows that austerity
Is good for others

And that hunger clearly must be
An aphrodisiac

Doesn't everyone know that neglect
Is a benign tumor

And that Americans
Eat too much anyway

Therefore it follows that some
Should eat nothing out of

A sense of patriotism
Everyone knows that only the lazy

Actually suffer
So watch these stick figures

Dancing quadrilles
And chanting their cult word

Malnutrition
Everyone knows an honest man

Shows his ribs
They're a kind of marimba in fact

Truly esthetic
And excellent for chamber music

Oh there is nothing like
The Bauhaus quality

Of the hollow cheek
And nothing quite as delightfully surreal

As a fat burgher's belly
Attached to a two-

Year-old
It's then of course everyone knows

That denial
Truly cleanses the spirit

Tonight, drinking wine full of shadows and sparks,
I remember an old porch and the evenings
we used so well under the the shade
of an ancient tree. That tree made the street a forest
and we sheltered there through sweet May
evenings, private and shadowy, incognito
on that street, finally rising clear of grief.
But one day men came and cut the tree down.
Joan shouted, "Tree murderers!" I seconded the motion
and the men looked puzzled, but the tree was gone
and we left the porch alone, every future evening
      cut down
with that ancient tree. But tonight I remember
the tree and that house and those years
gone to sawdust too, I suppose, and, as Pao would say,
I was seized by sorrow. Before they killed the tree
that porch was our own country, our pocket republic
whose frontiers only we could cross. Sometimes
we saw hummingbirds around the lilacs, precise
      as bees.
We loved those evenings as light drained toward chill
and neighbors disappeared to hone the blades
of their operatic mowers. Now other griefs
knock on the door, chainsaws ready, mowers growling,
but that porch is gone, that house is gone, those
      evenings

plowed under, only here and there sprouting
a beach daisy of memory. I cultivate them tonight
dreaming with the shadow wine, letting its leisure
uncover what it will, spark or shadow, porch or tree.
The summer is hot, the kind that drives Oregonians
crazy. That blue sky all day blinds them and they drive
their cars all night anywhere at all, around the block,
to mountain and sea looking for clouds, that safe
overcast, that subtle air of mist and river mixed.
But hot as it is I know the rich leaves now hanging
limp as old party decorations will fall and rustle
underfoot, and with Pao I take this as a loud
warning. He said life passes like lightning.
Remembering that porch I know the taste.
And in "Tedious Ways" he said dead leaves are dead
and we burn our youth to nothingness.
Pao, what can we say? I sit here at forty-four
feeling every day of every year, and that porch
and those days are near as ancient China.
There isn't time to compete against anyone, you said.
Pao, I live in a country where we compete
over who can eat too much, who can be most humble.
But in a language we can't understand, in words
most have forgotten, you said: Keep your noble aims,
enjoy your friends and wine, for only these
can keep worry and fear away. (God knows we try.
Just count our empties—bottles *and* friends.)
Then you added, with an elegance and irony
that makes us laugh, "You still look unhappy.

280   Don't you like my 'Tedious Ways'?" We do.
We do. Yet we have only these few poems—nothing
and everything—along with our own tedium and the
            crumbling
sense that too much fell when they slaughtered that tree,
as if the totem of some shadowy nobility
fell that day. But right now the wine is cool
and I honor you, knowing your life was as
tear-stained as anyone's, and your time and mine
could share a name: The Years of Madness, say.
Old comrade, we bridge a gap without a bridge
and I toast your ruined city with my own.
In fact, I'll match you town for town, desolate
tomb for tomb, dishonor for dishonor.
Both our bunches knew the tricks. You said
many died of poison at the River Ching, and crossing
the Lu you were lucky only to be ill.
I have your meaning and my rivers, too.
(Some east of here catch fire, most ooze along
having forgotten their old dance.) And my street
is a river. Across it a witch lives.
We are at perpetual silent war. Other nearby houses
seethe like teakettles with illegible hate,
steam whistling Need Need Need. Need chews
their owners inside-out. Their world batters them
to sleep at night, batters them awake.
The people think they thrive but wonder what is missing

and why their empire too falls to disrepair.
But you knew how glory had been stolen, a rich tooled
    life
lay back there somewhere before infancy. And once in
    your
ruined city carts and chariots rubbed axles
like men's shoulders. There was laughter and song
and the great glory of abundance, the glory
of too much, of teeming yields, but then the land
was cut up like a melon, shared out like beans
and glory ended in weeds. Pao, our cities
look bombed, greed grinds whole neighborhoods
away, buildings are pulled out like teeth
and the cellars yawn their craters to the moon.
We, too, hear of yields. Of abundance.
You said, the law of nature was the greatest
displeasure for the largest number; that for
a thousand miles only brown dust flew.
You listened to the silence of your ruined city
and couldn't believe how once, behind painted doors,
there was dancing and laughter and music
and rare fish and young girls fragrant as orchids—
and that all that, each song, each fish, each girl
now lay under stones. Pao Chao, we dig our stones
each day. In our music there is silence, in our cities
a brown dust falls. And our last stillness lies
just over the horizon, buzzing like a dial tone.